EQUAL MEASURES

Ethnic minority and bilingual pupils in secondary schools

EQUAL MEASURES

Ethnic minority and bilingual pupils in secondary schools

Edited by Penny Travers
and Gillian Klein

Trentham Books

Stoke on Trent, UK and Sterling, USA

Trentham Books Limited

Westview House	22883 Quicksilver Drive
734 London Road	Sterling
Oakhill	VA 20166-2012
Stoke on Trent	USA
Staffordshire	
England ST4 5NP	

First published 2004

British Library Cataloguing-in-Publication Data
A catalogue record for this book is available from the British Library

ISBN-13: 978-1-85856-303-9
ISBN-10: 1-85856-303-8

Designed and typeset by Trentham Print Design Ltd., Chester and printed in Great Britain by Bemrose Shafron (Printers) Ltd., Chester.

equal measures

affirmative action
A policy or a programme that seeks to redress past discrimination through active measures to ensure equal opportunity, as in education.

Idioms and phrases
www.gurunet.com

If you hear my need
Then hear too my unsung strength
In equal measure

Valerie Witonska

Acknowledgements
Our thanks to Enfield LEA for the initiatives which inspire and inform this book.

However, the views expressed or implied here are not to be understood as necessarily reflecting those of Enfield LEA. All the authors write in a personal capacity.

We also thank Shallum for letting us use the photograph of him discovering *Romeo and Juliet* for our cover.

Acknowledgements and thanks are also due to
Karnak House Publishers for the extract from *The fat black woman's poems*
Oxford University Press for 'The naming of parts' from *Collected Poems* (1991) by Henry Reed, edited by John Stallworthy

Contents

Foreword

Silvaine Wiles

In a recently published Ofsted report, one of the main findings was that creating an inclusive school required considerable effort and commitment. In successful schools, 'no stone was left unturned'.

It seems to me that one could say the same of Enfield LEA and, in particular, its team of Ethnic Minority Achievement advisers (also known as LCAS developments) within the School Improvement Service. Over the years this team, in cooperation with local schools and other LEA advisers, has built up a formidable national reputation for responding positively to the cultural and linguistic diversity of the local student population. The needs of minority ethnic and bilingual pupils are viewed as central to schools' policy making and provision, not an afterthought. For as long as I can remember, the LCAS stance has been one of inclusion, and its advisory work and action research projects have resulted, time and again, in quality publications, offering genuinely helpful advice for practitioners.

This publication is a new venture – written by members of the team together with LEA colleagues – and it is no exception. It records work in progress across a wide spectrum of educational challenge. It offers strategies for ensuring that the needs of underachieving groups are addressed, for ensuring that key government initiatives are translated into effective classroom practice for all pupils, for celebrating pupils' cultural and linguistic heritages, for confronting stereotyping and racism and for ensuring that the voices of pupils and their parents are heard. In brief, ways of ensuring that education becomes a joint venture between home and school so that individual strengths and talents are utilised to the full.

In the first contribution, Giang Vo (now an inner-city maths teacher) reflects on her schooling in this country. Two striking themes emerge: her recognition that despite 'speaking English like a trooper' at primary school, she still had some way to go if she were to use English with the precision and creativity needed to excel academically at secondary level, and secondly, her desire to blend in rather than stand out. My secondary school, she tells us, 'did not value my uniqueness. I was very unhappy and felt guilty that I was different.'

Can we be confident that such experiences are a thing of the past? If we adopt the inclusive practices described in this book, there would at least be grounds for optimism.

Preface

Penny Travers

I have crossed an ocean
I have lost my tongue.
From the root of the old one
A new one has sprung.

'Epilogue' by Grace Nichols
The fat black woman's poems
Virago 1984

An early working title for this book was 'Crossing an ocean'. The phrase seemed to capture so much that we were trying to communicate. In the prologue, Giang Vo describes a real ocean crossing from South Vietnam through international waters in the South China Sea in a desperate escape from oppression and a sense of being imprisoned in her own country. She literally lost or left behind a culture and way of life and had to acquire a new language in a different land. The subsequent chapters outline the various ways in which pupils are required to navigate their way through school and the curriculum. For ethnic minority and bilingual pupils in particular this can be a tough journey – especially at secondary level. They are required to move towards adulthood and succeed academically in an environment which they may or may not find supportive. For some, this involves working within a new culture. For others, success also has to be achieved in a new language. A difficult passage certainly, but 'crossing an ocean' seemed, ultimately, too cryptic and misleading – would ambitious seafarers seeking a practical manual be disappointed?

This book, nevertheless, does chart a journey taken by a group of practitioners working in multiethnic, multilingual schools in one particular London borough, Enfield, and committed to creating equal opportunities for all pupils. Its perspective is a broad and wide ranging and this is its particular strength. The writers offer their expertise and experience as advisers in teaching and learning, second language acquisition, raising ethnic minority achievement, anti racism, working with Eastern European Roma and refugee pupils and gifted and talented pupils. As the chapter titles indicate, all these areas are addressed. The many different groups of young people are considered and insights, learning and effective ways forward suggested. Here you will find proposals for including aspects of Roma culture and lifestyles within the curriculum and the opening lines from poems written by a group of pupils who took part in a Gifted and Talented project. There are comments from teachers about shifts they've made in their own thinking and practice and suggestions for bringing lessons alive through developing group work and talk. Ways of initiating pro-active whole school approaches to counter racism are outlined, along with strategic approaches to effective planning and classroom delivery. Teaching assistants talk with enthusiasm about their own learning and feedback from pupils. Most importantly, perhaps, pupils' voices are heard – pupils from ethnic minority groups who are not generally consulted and who, for a variety of reasons, are often silent. Here, a wish list from a group of Somali boys is included and the reflections of Roma parents are captured alongside the views and recommendations of a group of highly achieving pupils from African Caribbean backgrounds.

The writers share a geographical location, but the views captured are of interest and relevance to a wide audience of educational practitioners working in schools and classrooms everywhere.

Giang Vo came to Britain in 1979 as a refugee. She describes her personal experience of arriving and being welcomed into a primary school and also of moving on to secondary school where she learnt, painfully, that she was 'different'. Had she been encouraged to become a member of the school community and actively included in learning, she would have continued happily on her journey of achievement. Sadly, she was made to feel an outsider and had to deal with being bullied and ignored. Drawing on her own sense of self and her motivation and persistence she did make progress and succeed – she works now as a mathematics teacher in an inner city school – but her account of her years in secondary education make moving reading and give all of us working at Key Stages 3 and 4 much to think about and address.

The chapters that follow Giang's prologue attempt to respond to some of the issues that she highlights: issues of welcoming newly arrived students, inclusion in all aspects of school life, teacher expectations, effective support – and challenge – for ethnic minority students and those learning English as an additional language, strategic planning and the need for imaginative approaches to teaching, learning and building a sense of belonging.

The book begins with reflection on recent work on managing change. Deborah Thompson describes the hands-on approach she and other advisory colleagues have taken to supporting schools with the implementation of the Key Stage 3 Strategy. This has meant actively rethinking schemes of work and lesson plans to ensure that key questions are addressed and all pupils involved with learning.

In chapter 2, Lesley Higgs and I revisit partnership teaching and offer mini case studies of bilingual pupils who've clearly benefited from the scaffolding put in place to support the writing process in English.

Vasant Mahandru's chapter 'Fluent Maths' gives examples from classroom practice of ways in which pupils who are learning English as an additional language make sense of the tasks they're given. It offers practical strategies for developing language acquisition alongside mathematical understanding and pupils' personal interest in the curriculum.

In chapter 4 Janet Campbell considers the specifical role teaching assistants play in raising ethnic minority achievement, and identifies training and models of good practice at primary school that can be transferred to secondary settings.

The two following chapters address particular groups of pupils who are vulnerable or at risk of failing to realise their full potential. Much can be done to enhance the learning experiences of these pupils. Graham Went discusses the 'double whammy' faced by Roma pupils; Mala German reflects on her work with a group of Somali boys.

The insights and recommendations of a group of highly achieving pupils from African Caribbean backgrounds are recorded in chapters 7 and 8. These emerged from a local action research project which came to be called 'Striving to Succeed'. Alison Heap describes the factors that support these pupils in successful learning and Marcia Sinclair focuses particularly on links with parents and community.

The book concludes with a look by John Broadbent at providing for gifted and talented pupils and the issues that need to be considered when working with this group – particularly if they are from ethnic minority and bilingual backgrounds.

Throughout, the writers reflect on creating the conditions for learning in which *all* pupils have the chance to succeed. Equality and inclusion are, perhaps, not so much achieved as worked towards. We would like to thank all the pupils, teachers and managers with whom we've worked. They have taught us much, including the fact that there is always more to do, realise and explore – in our own thinking as well as in our practice. This publication is an account of work in progress, underpinned by a belief in the importance of creating the right conditions for learning and the hope that, were Giang to arrive in a secondary school today, her experience would be an affirming and positive one.

Prologue
Speaking from experience

Giang Vo

Recently I was asked to make a short film as part of a training package for non-teaching support staff in schools. I was asked how I felt as a refugee child coming to Great Britain and meeting the education system here for the first time. As I began to reminisce, some vivid memories came flooding back to me.

I arrived in Chepstow in summer 1979. I was immediately put into school along with my five cousins when term started, and I loved it. I had been an 'A' student in Vietnam and my expectations for my new school were very positive. I wanted to learn and I was confident that I would. I had no fear of the new school system and this gave me the springboard I needed to learn English really, really quickly.

I can best describe the way I learnt English as an absorption of the new world in which I found myself. I absorbed the language and the people. At school I was withdrawn for a short time during English lessons so that I could learn the basics of the language, and during the summer holiday, before I entered school, my cousins and I had extra English and maths lessons. This gave me a good grounding and some confidence in my ability to communicate. I was never withdrawn from any of the regular lessons, however, so I took geography, history, needlework etc with everyone else. It was in these lessons that I had a chance to put my newly acquired knowledge to the test. The desire to answer questions and understand the work about glaciers in geography and about the Saxons in history pushed me to use and expand my vocabulary. In maths I was miles ahead of everyone else but it allowed me to pick up the terminology. Similarly, the needlework classes allowed me to listen and sometimes join in with the conversation around the table. These classes were the perfect incubators for my language development. I learnt about 'knock knock' jokes and Dennis the Menace and a classmate even went so far as to profess his love to me during needlework! I don't think I could have found a better place not only to pick up the language but also to use it effectively, enabling me to integrate slowly into the school society.

There were other factors that also helped, such as the wonderful world of television. No matter if it was in black and white or colour, I was totally fascinated. You've got to realise that I'd just arrived from a country that survived on one feature programme a week, with the rest of the schedule filled with news and propaganda. I was immediately hooked on Batman and Robin, Spiderman, The Incredible Hulk ... you name it, I watched it. It wasn't surprising really that I learnt to speak English so quickly. I was desperate to understand what was happening on the screen and these programmes were direct in their deliveries. Most of my superheroes backed up their words with immediate actions so it didn't take long to deduce the meanings of most sentences. I also listened to the radio as I liked pop music. Listening to the songs on the radio and learning the lyrics helped me enormously.

Of course it wasn't all plain sailing. I didn't start waxing lyrical as soon as I arrived in Britain. On the contrary, it took me a while to pluck up my courage to say anything at all. At first I just wanted to listen. To hear how people pronounced certain words or how they would string their sentences together. And I didn't want to just listen once either. I had to hear sentences several times before I was confident enough that I had heard correctly. The way people speak to each other seemed to take precedence over anything I learnt out of a book. I'm not saying I didn't remember the things I'd learnt in lessons, it was just that I was more able to remember sentences spoken in the playground and more willing to repeat it to another friend. These sentences were more alive and accessible. They just seem cooler to use. And this proved to be true – when I used the sentence 'Hello, how are you?' in the playground it would often invite giggles amongst the few polite replies. But saying, 'Hey, what are you playing?' or 'Can I play?' would get me into the games. Learning rude words was also another great gimmick to gain you new friends. So I'm afraid I did this too, with gusto.

I was at school with five cousins but because we were split up and placed in different classes we had to learn to talk to the other kids. In the playground it was a different matter and it was a relief sometimes to hang around with people you know well again, especially in the early days when I could not speak English so well. And yes, we did gossip in our own language. But then didn't everybody, in English or otherwise?

I loved my primary school and strongly believe that my progress was made quicker because of the way I was treated. From day one there was total inclusion.

It was already obvious in terms of appearance that I was different from the other children. But the school allowed me to attend regular lessons. I was made to be part of my class's assembly play and Christmas play like everyone else. I was punished when naughty and praised when good. There were no concessions. I played netball and rounders with everyone and entered all the school competitions. I even won a few. Since I felt that I was on equal par with everyone else it gave me the confidence to behave like everyone else, and ultimately I tried to speak and learn like everyone else.

In secondary school several aspects in my life changed. By then I was speaking English like a trooper and was an 'A' student so the safety net of support which had always given me the confidence I needed was taken away. I no longer received support in English and teachers started expecting me to always excel. There were expectations placed upon me by my parents and teachers to perform and integrate and because I was conformist and studious I was expected to achieve even more than my peers. People observed my ability to communicate orally and my academic achievements and assumed that I was on an equal footing with the rest of the children my age. The truth was that my family and I understood very little about the British system and my parents were unable to do something as simple as choose a good secondary school for me. So I enrolled into what felt, at that time, like one of the most difficult secondary schools in inner London.

I guess the biggest difference about learning in secondary school was that it was no longer so much fun. Grades and expectations were more and more important. And now learning English was no longer as natural as breathing. The years of picking up English as a way of communicating were superseded by a time of needing to know about the exactness and lyrical qualities of the English language and also its beauty. I had picked up the idiosyncrasies easily as I lived the language every day, using it in my daily life. I now needed to be taught about grammar and punctuation, alliteration and simile. I started to learn to express myself in a more flamboyant and creative way. But too soon schooling ended; now I have forgotten many things.

Secondary school was a very threatening environment for me. I still remember my experience there with dread. All it provided was a stepping stone, a place where you gained grades, a springboard from which to move on to better and brighter things. Why did I not come out of school a more rounded and more confident individual? Well I guess, like everyone else who was a millimetre outside the 'norm band', I was picked on at school for being different. My command of the English language did not help me here. In fact it might have been better if I had not understood some of the comments thrown my way. I was desperate for people to understand about me and where I came from. The stereotypes and ignorant comments were never challenged. Not by me – I was too scared. And definitely not by the school. The bullying carried on in the corridors and classrooms and I think the teachers too were under attack. Every time I was bullied I wanted to explain myself, to tell people about my life and why I was in this country. I carried with me stories and feelings and a great sense of pride about my country and my people. I was proud of my struggles and being brave every single day in this new country. But I never had the chance to explain. Mostly children, but adults too seemed to think I did not exist before coming to England, and made me felt ashamed of the past. They made me think that I only became a whole human being, civilised, when I stepped onto these shores. In the end I stopped wanting to express myself. I thought people would never understand and would only laugh at the differences in me. I wanted to blend into the background; I wanted the bliss that I thought would come if I was no longer different. It never came.

When refugees come to Britain they do not only have to deal with their own emotional baggage but also with the emotional baggage of their hosts. This is often a forgotten fact. When I arrived in Britain as a boat person there was already so much media interest and dissection about my people, all of which I was oblivious to yet all of which I would have to face in some way. I faced ignorance not only from children but from teachers too. I think most adults were afraid to discuss my situation for fear of bringing up some disturbing memories. So instead, while some of my teachers mistakenly believed I was traumatised by the Vietnam War, others did not know where Vietnam was. Some of my classmates revelled in telling me that dogs were part of my regular diet and that I must have enjoyed the privilege of meeting Rambo.

When people talk about refugees and immigrants they often focus on the problems they bring. No one concentrates on how we can best use the talents and experience that these people bring. Few people think about our need to explain ourselves.

In primary school I felt people wanted to know about me and wanted to be my friend because I was different. They enjoyed the different games I introduced to them. I was happy, communicative and creative then. In secondary school I felt people did not want me. They thought I was beneath them; they did not value my uniqueness. I was very unhappy and felt guilty that I was different.

I was pleased to be asked to write this piece as I know that things in schools, particularly in secondary schools, could be better for ethnic minority and bilingual pupils. As a teacher myself now, I do what I can – I think – to create a welcoming and exciting classroom. The chapters that follow give us stories, ideas and guidance on what more we can do.

1

Transforming Key Stage 3: securing real change in secondary schools

Deborah Thompson

I used to hate doing the industrial revolution. We got bogged down in Spinning Jennies and tarmac. This new approach really engaged pupils' interest. They all got involved and understood the big key changes. (Head of History department in a multilingual secondary school in challenging circumstances.)

These words are testimony to the success of implementing the Key Stage 3 Strategy; of re-thinking planning, lesson structure and teaching approaches. This chapter is a reflection on the process and practicalities of managing change. It offers insights into what needs to happen inside and outside classrooms to make a difference.

When the cross-curricular literacy strand of the Key Stage 3 Strategy was introduced in 2001, our experience as a literacy team (consultants within the School Improvement Service working together with EMA advisers) was that teachers in secondary schools reacted with considerable enthusiasm. The training modules clearly promoted good practice and offered teaching strategies which addressed widely acknowledged problems. After borough wide and school based training days, heads of department in the secondary schools undertook exhaustive and exhausting audits. These revealed that many pupils, as expected, struggled with literacy and needed to develop skills in listening, speaking, reading and especially writing. Whole school literacy targets such as 'Enable pupils to develop accurate use of paragraphing and punctuation', were identified and placed strategically on staffroom and classroom walls, alongside the ever-lengthening lists of key words. They were then largely ignored.

There were several reasons for this disappointing outcome. Despite attending the training days which focused on core strategies, in particular the vital skills of active reading and the teacher modelling of writing, many teachers did not fully understand how language is used in their subject areas to make use of the targets. Even when they were conversant with the requisite language structures and subject specific vocabulary, they often could not make these explicit to their pupils.

By the end of the first year of the strategy, it was clear that the initiative had largely stalled. All that remained was a somewhat mechanical listing of key words at the start of a lesson. The exceptions to this depressing picture were the schools which were already confident in their literacy development work or which had received intensive support, tailored to the needs and circumstances of particular departments.

Staffrooms and departmental offices across the country are now stacked with folders produced by the Key Stage 3 Strategy. Each new folder represents a further development and refinement of the best practice promoted in the earliest modules. A common reaction to this deluge has been a feeling of being hopelessly overwhelmed, followed by a defensive response to any proposals for development. The Foundation Subject strand, introduced in 2002, depends for success on raising attainment in literacy. The training modules exemplify good practice and reaffirm many of the core strategies included in the original cross curricular literacy training. The evidence is, however, that without direct and tailored support for schools, this training is having as little impact as the original modules, whatever their intrinsic quality.

In order to change practice in secondary schools significantly, hard pressed subject leaders need focused help to identify and apply the core principles within their departments. It is challenging, in terms of both time and experience, to apply the generic principles of the strategy to individual subject areas. Plus there is often in-built resistance, linked to earlier literacy initiatives. Previously, teachers were often encouraged to deliver what were essentially English lessons, dropped into their schemes of work: for example, a lesson on the features of persuasive text as part of a unit on town planning. This approach caused some resentment and drew accusations that the broader curriculum was seen primarily as a vehicle for teaching literacy. The chances of success were further undermined by teachers' lack of confidence in their ability to teach these skills and the obvious time constraints under which all schools operate.

If schools are to undertake and successfully embed change, the process has to be made manageable. First and foremost, the flood of material emanating from the DfES has to be reduced to a short, coherent set of key principles, to be embedded systematically within the planning and practice of individual departments. All the training modules, both Cross Curricular and Foundation Subject, rest on a set of core strategies. Unless schools have these in place, standards are unlikely to improve, and further development is virtually impossible.

The core strategies can be simply articulated as:

- objective driven planning
- the three or four part lesson with effective plenary
- teacher modelling of speaking, listening, reading and writing
- inclusive, interactive, multisensory, talk based teaching and learning strategies, particularly important in multilingual schools.

Once they have identified these key approaches and strategies, departments need targeted support to apply them to their own practice. It is essential that the aims and objectives of the support are fully understood and supported by senior managers, and integrated into the school's development plan. Initially, this support demands a real commitment from the school in terms of teacher release time. Ongoing monitoring and evaluation by the senior management is required to imbue the initiative with the high status essential for success.

Our starting point for working with schools is to review planning with individual heads of department and, where possible, other key staff. It has proved helpful to undertake this work in light of the Foundation Subjects strand and from the perspective of effective strategies for inclusion. In our authority, intensive support schools all have a high percentage of pupils learning English as an additional language, and meeting their needs is fundamental to successful teaching and learning. However, by treating EAL inclusion as a separate consideration, there is a real risk of a bolt-on approach. What is needed, on the contrary, is for the literacy demands of every lesson automatically to be taken into account so as to support, challenge and include all the pupils. The approach we promote meets these needs and, because it is good practice, it effectively fosters all pupils' learning.

Many of the heads of department with whom we worked as an LEA team took the opportunity radically to revise their schemes of work. In reality, many departments had wholly inadequate medium and short term planning. The need for more detailed, developed planning is particularly acute given the large number of non-specialists and overseas-trained teachers currently working at Key Stage 3. Heads of department were aware that this planning would be invaluable in helping them support new or inexperienced staff, particularly if they also ensured that comprehensive and reusable resource packs were produced for each member of staff.

The initial question we pose when reviewing a unit of work relates to the key strategy principle of objective driven planning. Much medium term planning is historic. The origins of particular units are lost in the mists of time but the worksheets are faithfully reproduced every year, so people continue to use them. This is particularly likely to happen in Foundation Subjects at Key Stage 3, simply because they are non-examination courses. Understandably, the limited time available for curriculum development tends to be focused on examination groups. This means there are history units where Year 8 pupils are colouring in pictures of Henry VIII's wives or selected Norman castles, and Year 9 geography plans which involve colouring a map of Brazil that names two towns and one river. The obvious question is why? Many units go into great detail in terms of activities – usually textbook or worksheet related – but pay scant attention to the key skills, knowledge and understanding they are intended to deliver.

Once the purpose for the intended learning is clearly established, the whole issue of inclusive planning and teaching can be explored. And this encompasses the entire literacy agenda. Working through specific units of work, it is possible to apply the core principles of the Strategy to real lessons, meeting the particular needs of a school's cohort. This also offers an unrivalled opportunity to clear up misunderstandings and challenge prejudices about the Strategy. Every lesson in the focus unit is planned in detail, with literacy to the fore – as fundamental to access and inclusion. In this way, literacy assumes its proper place as a key skill, serving and being reinforced in all curriculum work.

It is clear from the sequence of work reproduced at the end of this chapter that there is an explicit focus on developing visual prompts – paintings, photographs and videos – to support the development of a meaningful understanding of subject specific vocabulary and to promote the use of speculative and inferential language. This approach attracted favourable comment when it was used in the science lesson shown in 'All Inclusive', module 12 of the initial cross curricular training but, in our experience, it was rarely implemented until concrete examples were developed for specific lessons. For example, Year 9 pupils beginning work on the industrialisation of Britain are asked to annotate a map of Britain in 1720, recording what they can see, infer and would like to ask. The collaborative, visual nature of the task makes it accessible to all pupils. Key vocabulary is introduced or reinforced in relation to a concrete activity, rather than as a de-contextualised list. Pupils at an early stage of learning English are clearly supported by an exploration of vocabulary, exemplified by a visual, sometimes physical activity.

> It's really helped that we have taken on these approaches across the school. Pupils have become expert at interrogating visual and media texts and using talk to focus on the content and language features of their writing. (History teacher)

Considerable use is made of physical activity to model particular vocabulary or key concepts. Lesson starters in science, physical education and technology frequently involve a physical response. Pupils may be asked to hold up cards, stand up or raise an arm to indicate which substances in a list are gases, for example. In history and religious education, pupils are asked to form human time lines and arrange key figures, represented by masks, along their length, before recording them on a worksheet. Obviously this kinaesthetic approach has been promoted by the strategy, but without encouragement to develop it in relation to the specific units they are delivering, most teachers will not take it on.

Teacher modelling is at the heart of Strategy pedagogy. However it is evident that many teachers are nervous and confused about what is meant by it. To be effective models as speakers, readers and writers, teachers need to have an analytical awareness and understanding of the specific language requirements of their subject specialism. As a part of the support offered, we have developed a range of planned speaking and listening activities, including classroom drama, which are built in to the planning and modelled by consultants where necessary. We include details of how teachers might use active reading strategies to annotate texts and provide a sample annotated text. Crucially, we provide annotated scripts for teachers to use when modelling writing particular text types.

Dedicating consultant support time to working with teachers to develop approaches which may be new and challenging is time well spent. This support is essential if the activity is not to take the form of unfocused shared writing, with little understanding of key success criteria for the task. The initial unit of work cannot be too detailed. It has to serve as a model for all that is to come. It needs to be self-explanatory and fully resourced. Teachers using it must experience success if they are to develop and extend their practice in the long as well as the short term. The benefits of working in partnership have been well documented by Hart (1991) and Levine (1990). Interestingly, Ofsted's *Managing the ethnic minority achievement grant. Good practice in secondary schools* (2004) cites partnership teaching as one of the most effective forms of whole school continuing professional development, referring to mainstream and EMA staff working collaboratively. The principle of working in partnership applies equally to consultants or advisers working with schools.

In many schools, problematic pupil behaviour is offered as the justification for employing a severely restricted range of teaching and learning styles. Copying and colouring are often strategies teachers use as defensive strategies for behaviour management. The use of collaborative, interactive approaches based on visual texts or drama techniques can seem too risky. Our experience is that when teachers are prepared to take the risk, the improvement in the pupils' behaviour is almost instantaneous. Our willingness to model or team teach these lessons is a huge factor in gaining the support and respect of the colleagues with whom we work. We have overwhelming evidence of the benefit even newly arrived pupils who are at the earliest stages of learning English derive from this approach. The use of visual resources, and drama techniques that give physical expression to both concrete and abstract vocabulary, enables them to be fully involved in the lesson and begin to make essential social contacts with classmates.

Once the initial unit of work has been planned, resourced and written up, it is important that the head of department and adviser are both allocated adequate time in which to share and discuss the work fully with the whole department. The head of department or lead teacher has to be prepared to take a leading role in delivering and evaluating the new unit, and to work in partnership with the adviser to support other colleagues. It is essential that enough time is allowed for reviewing and revising the unit, once it has been delivered.

From an adviser's perspective, a major indication of success is that the responsibility for the development of second and subsequent units of work shifts to the class teachers. Ideally, the head of department should take the main responsibility for developing these further units, involving other department members, with the adviser checking the quality and possibly polishing the outcomes. The investment of time in developing the initial unit can only be justified if ownership of the process passes rapidly to an energised and empowered department.

It has been our experience that teachers value the process itself, once they have overcome any initial anxiety about it. Above all, they welcome the opportunity to spend a significant amount of time reflecting on their subject and professional practice. Teachers particularly value the way we acknowledge the inevitable difficulties in successfully including all pupils, and place this consideration at the heart of the planning. The fact that senior managers have provided designated time for preparation and reflection also makes staff feel valued and appreciated.

The role of the adviser shifts as the process continues. This external consultant no longer leads, but rather encourages and reassures the head of department and provides practical support for weaker or less experienced staff. It is vital that successes are celebrated and shared, within the department and across the school. In the schools where this work has become embedded, the triumphs of the departments undertaking it have been well publicised by senior managers. These departments have been able to act as a model for others within the school and for other schools in the LEA. All the schools involved have impressive classroom displays of pupils' work, reflecting the talk based and collaborative nature of many of the tasks. These displays are real work in progress as opposed to polished, finished pieces – for example an enlarged portrait of two historical characters with post-its or speech bubbles added to suggest their differing thoughts and perspectives.

Every department that has taken on the revision of their Key Stage 3 curriculum described has also employed the range of core teaching and learning strategies within Key Stages 4 and 5. The core principles and strategies soon begin to inform practice across the whole department, developing a common, consistent approach to teaching and learning. This benefits all the pupils and they become increasingly comfortable with this extended range of teaching and learning strategies.

Once the planning is in place, it is important that teachers have time to deliver it, familiarise themselves with the strategies, make mistakes and generally get to grips with the approach, without coming under scrutiny while they are doing so. Any outside involvement should be entirely supportive, for example modelling or team teaching with the consultant or head of department. However once the new approach has had time to embed, usually about half a term, it is imperative that the head of department, adviser and senior managers carry out a rigorous programme of monitoring and evaluation to assess the impact on pupil achievement. The outcomes of this process will determine the next steps for the department and the school. In particular it will identify which pupils need additional support and which are in a position to act as role models for their peers.

There is no quick fix solution to the problems faced by secondary schools when they try to implement change. Most teachers, including even really effective middle managers, are too busy to engage with the mass of material which lands on their desks. Those of us who have the opportunity to focus on a key aspect of pedagogy and practice can best help our school based colleagues by sifting and summarising the key principles and strategies known to contribute to raising standards in education. We must then invest time and our expertise in applying them specifically to the needs and circumstances of individual schools. If we offer schools generalised, non-specific principles, these will be quietly ignored. If departments are presented with principles and practical strategies which demonstrably work, they will embrace them and truly transform teaching and learning.

With thanks to Noel Frayn and Ruth Fairburn and their departments, and to Annie Powell and her History department.

Unit 1: How did William the Conqueror succeed in conquering and remaining King of England?

Learning Objectives	Possible teaching activities	Learning Outcomes	Points to note
Pupils recognise use of chronology in creating order in History	**Starter** Pupil quiz, cards displaying a variety of historical figures (Moses, Christ, Mohamed, Julius Caesar, Alfred the Great, William the Conqueror, Robin Hood, HenryV111, Queen Victoria, Guy Fawkes, Winston Churchill, Martin Luther King, Mary Seacole) pupils have to identify them and suggest dates.Spend two minutes in pairs. Feedback, agree identity and dates **Core Activity** Class in playground. Pupils given a card naming a figure Pupils arrange themselves in chronological order They estimate space between their neighbours, using rope (1 metre = 100 years) according to dates on their cards Pupil learning is re-enforced by completing worksheet. Figures entered in correct order and place on timeline **Plenary** Teachers sets half-term biography homework	Pupils demonstrate their ability to place historical dates and information in correct chronological order	**Key Question (KQ)**: What use are dates in History? **Key Skill (KS)**: Chronology **Key Words(KW)**: chronology, sequencing, order, arrange, dates

Unit 1: How did William the Conqueror succeed in conquering and remaining King of England? continued

Learning Objectives	Possible teaching activities	Learning Outcomes	Points to note
Pupils understand that events take place in history for identifiable reasons	**Starter** Recap on previous lesson. Pupils shown three groups of invaders (Romans /Saxons /Vikings) with dates in chronological order, Place them on whole class enlarged version of lesson 1 timeline **Core Activity** In groups, pupils are given picture of invaders in a representative setting (Roman general in city of Rome, Saxon farmer in bleak landscape, Viking invader in full armour) plus list of possible reasons for invasion (slaves, fertile land, silver/tin, glory, plunder). In pairs, pupils decide which reasons would be most important for each invader and why. What do they already know? What can they see and infer from the picture? In groups of three, pupils form tableaux and strike a pose as one of the three invaders. Each invader gives one special reason why his people invaded England. Pupils have a worksheet with the three characters, complete statements for each invading group (could be homework). Some pupils should be expected to give reasons, 'We need slaves because....' **Plenary** Pupils agree which reasons are common to all invaders and which are particularly important to one or other invaders and why	Pupils use drama techniques to demonstrate historical understanding	**KQ**: Why was Britain invaded? **KS**: Causation **KW**: causes, reasons, tableaux, invasions, settlement, Empire

Unit 1: How did William the Conqueror succeed in conquering and remaining King of England? continued

Learning Objectives	Possible teaching activities	Learning Outcomes	Points to note
Pupils identify note-taking as a research tool	**Starter:** In pairs, identify homelands of Romans, Saxons, and Vikings on map of Europe **Core Activity** Introduction to England in 1065/6 by showing Simon Schama video in small chunks. Note-taking modelled by teacher. Clarify key questions / information to be identified from video, e.g Was England a united country in 1066? What was the Danelaw? Who were the different peoples living in England? Was England a Christian country?) Watch video through once. Watch again, model note taking process. Allow pupils to practise on next small chunk, check progress. Complete note taking. Check and agree key points. Teacher models writing first part of paragraph to describe England in 1065/6. Offer prompts to pupils who need support, such as sentence starters or pictures. **Plenary** Pupils feed back on what they have learnt about England in 1065/6	Pupils demonstrate the ability to make notes for research purposes	**KQ**: What was England like before 1066 **KS**: Enquiry **KW**: Note-taking/ modelling/research

Unit 1: How did William the Conqueror succeed in conquering and remaining King of England? continued

Learning Objectives	Possible teaching activities	Learning Outcomes	Points to note
Pupils empathise with an historical figure	**Starter** Pictures and names of claimants board and A3 sheet. In pairs, pupils annotate sheet. What do they see and what can they infer from pictures (warriors, ambitions, ethnic origin, etc)? **Core Activity** Active reading exercise on 3 claimants from resource sheet. Teacher models text marking and noting key information about Hardrada's claim, exploring meaning of key words in context. Pupils extract key information about Harold and William in mixed ability pairs. Record in books. Main points of all three claims noted on sugar paper for class record/display. Pupils create frozen picture of Harold swearing allegiance to William. In groups of 4, two represent what H and W say, two represent what H and W are thinking. Teacher models writing Hardrada's manifesto. Pupils write manifesto for Harold or William. Those at early stages of learning English complete one or more speech bubbles for claimant (2 lessons) **Plenary** Pupils discuss which claim is strongest and vote for preferred candidate by secret ballot	Pupils demonstrate an understanding of claims to throne through speech making	**KQ**: Who should be King? **KS**: Empathy **KW**: Heir/succession/right election

Unit 1: How did William the Conqueror succeed in conquering and remaining King of England? continued

Learning Objectives	Possible teaching activities	Learning Outcomes	Points to note
Pupils use historical knowledge to predict outcome	**Starter** Recap claims to throne through class record. Result of class vote announced **Core Activity** Pupils annotate comparison sheet of Norman and Saxon strengths/weaknesses. Which factors are most significant and why? In pairs, pupils design questions for 'hot-seating' Norman/Saxon baron/ thane Teacher in role to begin with. Pupils come into hot seat as appropriate. Come out of role as necessary to evaluate quality of answers. What evidence is there for Norman/ Saxon view of their own positions? **Plenary** If you had been writing a newspaper article in 1006, who would you have predicted would win and why? Agree key points for class display/record	Pupils conduct interview and make prediction	**KQ**: Who was best prepared for battle at Hastings in 1066? **KS**: Enquiry **KW**: resources, weapons, support , money/finance

Unit 1: How did William the Conqueror succeed in conquering and remaining King of England? continued

Learning Objectives	Possible teaching activities	Learning Outcomes	Points to note
Pupils are aware that historians ask key questions of sources to reach a conclusion	**Starter** Categorise information as primary or secondary evidence. Give pupils examples of reports, interviews, videos etc. What makes evidence more or less reliable, biased? **Core Activity** Evaluate Bayeux Tapestry, through Power point presentation, as historical source. What are the key points made by Normans in their account of their victory? Focus on death of Harold in Bayeux tapestry and teacher models source evaluation Source work activity given to class **Plenary** Show Schama Video of Battle scenes. How does this modify the Norman version of their victory? Probably two lessons	Pupils use a primary historical source to make inference about a historical event	**KQ**: Who won the Battle of Hastings? **KS**: Interpretation **KW**: Bayeux tapestry, historical source, primary, secondary, provenance, bias, reliability

Unit 1: How did William the Conqueror succeed in conquering and remaining King of England? continued

Learning Objectives	Possible teaching activities	Learning Outcomes	Points to note
Pupils identify the role of the monarchy in Medieval Government	**Starter** A3 sheet. Picture of Queen, P.M. and Houses of Parliament in centre. In pairs, pupils annotate to record areas of responsibility for modern government. Use picture prompts to stimulate (roads, hospitals, schools, army, justice system, tax collection, homeless etc, farms, factories.) Discuss extent of government role and largely ceremonial function of queen **Core Activity** Pupils given picture of William the Conqueror What would be the expectations of him in role as king? What would be the same / different from modern government? Record key aspects of role on post-its, with reason, prioritise (keeping the peace, defence, conquest, justice, tax collection). Each pair/group stick post-its around class picture. Which aspect of role is most important and why? **Plenary** Teacher models writing job description for medieval king. Pupils to complete own description for HW. Give pro-forma. Physical characteristics, personality, skills/ abilities	Pupils demonstrate understanding of the role of a King	**KQ**: Why was a King important in the Middle Ages? **KS**: Organisation and communication **KW**: king, monarchy, job, role, authority

Unit 1: How did William the Conqueror succeed in conquering and remaining King of England? continued

Learning Objectives	Possible teaching activities	Learning Outcomes	Points to note
Pupils aware of role of feudalism in structure of ordered Government in Middle Ages	**Starter** Pupils explore the idea of hierarchy through organising pictures of members of school community, most to least powerful. What are the powers and responsibilities of each tier? **Core Activity** Use a variety of picture and text based sources to understand how William used land as a reward to secure loyalty and extend Norman control across England. Refer specifically to king, barons, knights/lords of manor, peasants. In groups of four, pupils form frozen picture using levels and space to show relationship between these four types. Classmates have to guess who is who. Pupils then have to utter a thought aloud for their character. Pupils create their own diagram to explain the essence of the feudal system (could be homework) **Plenary** Agree a key statement to sum up position of each key section of feudal society. Consider how the church would fit in to this system	Pupils demonstrate understanding of feudal system in simple writing frame	**KQ**: How did William make sure he was obeyed? **KS**: Knowledge and understanding **KW**: obey, duty, feudal, feudalism

Unit 1: How did William the Conqueror succeed in conquering and remaining King of England? continued

Learning Objectives	Possible teaching activities	Learning Outcomes	Points to note
Pupils identify taxation as source of Government revenue	**Starter:** Pay packet OHP: what does it show? Link back to roles of government starter. What does tax, National Insurance pay for? **Core Activity** Introduce Domesday Book through video. Why does William need to have this information? Recap on roles lesson. What will king need money for? How will he know who to tax and how much? Look at info in book about Enfield/Edmonton Teacher models extracting/ recording key info. Pupils work on other extracts independently Pupils use sources to compare revenues available What does the book tell us about English society and economy? **Plenary** Pupils feed back on results of comparison. Clarify how this information would benefit William	Pupils demonstrate ability to extract key information from source	**KQ**: How did William become rich from his new Kingdom? **KS**: Enquiry **KW**: Taxes, finance, wealth, Domesday Book

Unit 1: How did William the Conqueror succeed in conquering and remaining King of England? continued

Learning Objectives	Possible teaching activities	Learning Outcomes	Points to note
Pupils identify the Castle as an important means of control in medieval England	**Starter** Pictures of three types of castles to place in chronological order and give reason for order. Each pair to offer a reason for Norman castle building. **Core Activity** Teacher introduces and models active reading strategies to extract info. on reasons for castle building Introduce research project and resources **Plenary** Feedback on ideas for research	Pupils embark on structured castle project as an independent study	**KQ**: How did the Normans control the Saxons? **KS**: Enquiry **KW**: research, motte and bailey, square keep, concentric, defence, attack

2

Beyond the naming of parts
Working with pupils at Key Stages 3 and 4 in the English curriculum

Penny Travers and Lesley Higgs

Today we have naming of parts. Yesterday,
We had daily cleaning. And tomorrow morning,
We shall have what to do after firing. But today,
Today we have naming of parts. Japonica
Glistens like coral in all of the neighbouring gardens,
And today we have naming of parts.
Lessons of the war, Part 1 'Naming of parts' by Henry Reed*

This chapter considers the ways in which teachers working in partnership can think and plan together to make the mainstream classroom a place where all pupils, including those new to English, can explore ideas and texts and express themselves with confidence.

Year 9, Autumn term, English, preparation for the SATs Shakespeare paper, *Romeo and Juliet*. Pupils are asked to write a summary of the story so far in their own words. Chlève, newly arrived from the Democratic Republic of Congo produces the piece in Figure 1 overleaf.

What does he shows us here?

He has a good grasp of the main events and key players in Act 1 and almost takes on the character of the prince as he expresses his indignation: 'Aren't you ashamed of fighting like that – you ought to be ashamed of yourselves you

* By permission of Oxford University Press.

Romeo and Juliet

Two familes çe batted for auquine ressont.
Alour le prince arrived est dit. Vous navez...
pas ontte des vous batte vous devez
avoir ontte Montogues est vous capulets.
Le prince leur dit arengele probleme de
mon retour. Saudin du caté des Montogues
un jeune boy saure du faulle called Romeo
Romeo va parle avec son amie ~~def~~ qui
s appel Mercutio .... Saudin un amie de
Romeo vun parle de une invitation d'un
ball Mas~~ked~~ked qui alieu chez le capulets.
Romeo est çe two friend deside ~~der~~
deseradre au balle Masked. Le soire
IL serant au balle Masked avec çe two
friend's Alour saproche la young girl
home Juliet.

Figure 1

Montagues and you Capulets' (translation of Chlève's writing). He is able to construct a piece of narrative writing in one of his languages, French, though he often writes phonetically – spelling words as they sound in speech, or as he has seen similar sounding words spelt:

> '*Vous navez pas ontte*' for *honte* – shame,
>
> '*Un jeune boy saure*' for *sort* – comes out.
>
> '*deside deseradre au balle masked*' – for *décident de se rendre* – decide to go to.

He includes English vocabulary where he knows it. While incomplete and inaccurate, this is a clear and lively piece of writing, including direct speech; it communicates knowledge and understanding of the early part of the play.

Eighteen months later, Chlève works on his first GCSE assignment, Writing to inform, explain, describe – autobiography. He writes about his grandfather (see Figures 2 and 3).

It is worth looking closely at what Chlève communicates here – both in his first draft and his polished version. Chlève writes in English now, inviting the reader into a simple, personal and moving account. He creates an arresting opening and, on redrafting, has crafted paragraphs, each describing an aspect or memory of his grandfather. He repeats words and phrases to help himself structure his writing; this device works effectively here, giving the piece a poetic quality. He has had a go at writing in the past tense though, as his first draft shows, he is still learning the English tense system and he will also need to be supported in developing a more varied and extensive vocabulary.

Chlève has made remarkable progress. He is an articulate, able student, keen to learn. He has also been supported and challenged in the steps he's made. He has been provided with opportunities to work collaboratively, have access to artefacts, visual resources, to read and analyse models of fluent writing and make use of prompts. Above all, perhaps, he's been noticed, his strengths recognised and he has been given 'scaffolding' in the form of frameworks and feedback (sometimes in French). A relationship has developed between Chlève and his teachers and other pupils, enabling learning and language development to happen.

'Human relationships are at the heart of schooling' writes Jim Cummins:

> The interactions that take place between students and teachers and among students are more central to student success than any method for teaching literacy, or science or math. (1996)

We as teachers need to ensure that we get to know our pupils and value and include their experiences of communities, cultures, language learning. This chapter guidare

When I was born I never know
dis will happen to me I never
know one day I will lost my
grand dad. My grand dad was
a person how have a good
heart. Same time I (will) membered
when I was yeung, my mather and
my father used to tell me I looked
like my grand dad. My grand
dad was a person who liked
singing (some) songs and play is guitar.
I (will) bember went I was six year
old my grand dad used to sing a
song (and) in that song (he) say
sayed one day I will get a
new life in a new world.
Same time went I sing a song and
danced. Them my mather sayed
to me "I will member went I was
went your grand dad was alive, I
used to see him dancing and
singing but it's all an old membery.
Sometimes I feel sorry for my self
because I [illegible]

I lost my grand dad and I don't
have one like evry one else. But I
know went I wanted him
the only place I can find him
is in my heart. My grand father
died in a car accident on the way to
the hospital. I could'nt believe my
grand father died in a car accident.
But soon I knew it was true I
lost my grand father. But now my
mather was right. When I look at
her face all I could see was
sadness and I looked at my brother
and my sister and soon I knew I
would be sad because
I lost my grand father.
I wasn't sad because I was
thinking about the song my
grand father was singing and
I believe my grand father
went in a new world like
on his song. I took his guitar
in and put in my house and
the guitar is the only memory
I got left of him.

Figure 2

9.2.99

The memory of my grand father

when I was born I never knew that this would happen to me. I never know that one day I will lost my grand dad.
My grand dad was a person who had a good heart,
At the same time I remembered when I was yong and my mother and father used to tell me that I looked like my grand dad.
My grand dad was a person who liked singing songs and playing his guitar I remember when I was six years old my grand dad used to sing a song.
In that song it said that one day I will get a new life in a new world.
some time went by and I sung a song and danced.
Then my mother said to me "I remember went I was young when your grand dad was alive, I used to see him dancing and singing but it is all an old membory.
Some time I feel sorry for my self

Figure 3

looks at how the naming of parts (at the level of text and genre and the structure of English – grammar, word choices, spelling) needs to be addressed while fostering pupils' individual voices and unique and creative expression. Students need to know what to do before, during and after reading a text to engage with it and make sense of it. They must also learn how to construct their own accurate and effective sentences and paragraphs. At the same time, they must have opportunities to glisten – to surprise and delight us with their insights and phrasing, to state as Chlève does that 'one day I will get a new life in a new world'.

Much of what we, as colleagues working together, say here is not new but we are keen to offer our conviction – and proof! – that the process of planning for *all* pupils works to the benefit of each and every pupil. One of our main approaches is to plan *backwards*, that is to think about the outcome we're setting out for our students to achieve and then plan the series of steps that lead to it.

So, for example, when we consider what makes for good autobiographical writing, we come up with the following:

- an individual voice
- expression of feelings as well as thoughts
- a good story, engaging narrative
- powerful expression
- clarity
- well structured writing, use of paragraphing and a variety of accurate sentence types and lengths.
- a sense of cohesion, unity of theme and tone.

We would want all pupils at all levels, including those still developing their literacy skills or new to English as well as those deemed to be gifted and talented, to meet these criteria. The challenge for us is to enable them to do so. We need to find models of good autobiographical writing by authors from varied backgrounds, including examples of work in languages other than English where possible and appropriate. We must develop pupils' study of effective writing and we need to offer our own experience and expertise, including our personal attempts at drafting analytical and creative ideas. Having shown pupils exactly how to construct texts, we then need to move them on to doing it alone, developing themselves as independent learners, readers, writers.

Some of the key principles which guide the work of the Key Stage 3 Strategy are particularly relevant here:

> Including all pupils in a culture of high expectations (no child left behind)
> Promoting assessment for learning (making every child special)
> (*From Practice and pedagogy*, 2003)

The guidance from the Strategy on what good teaching looks like has also been helpful, as it spells out the importance of engagement, structure and challenge. The detailed deconstruction of the writing process has been especially useful. We are clearer now about the need to address the study of writing at text, sentence and word level and to be much more explicit about modelling what good writers – and readers – do. Those of us working with bilingual pupils have always brought our knowledge of language acquisition and English grammar to our planning and teaching with mainstream colleagues. We now have some clear, accessible models to support the process of reading for meaning and to teach the craft of writing. The 'writing sequence' offered by the Strategy is a powerful tool for introducing different genres – both fiction and non-fiction – to pupils. Used not as a rigid framework but as a prompt sheet, it provides a guide to constructing a piece of written work. It highlights the importance of looking closely at examples and exploring the particular features and defining the conventions of a text type. So in addition to looking at models of powerful writing, and considering content and style as we do when working on autobiography, we now examine explicitly the structure and grammar of these kinds of text. The grid (see Figure 4) shows pupils' comments on different autobiographical extracts they have read.

They identify key themes, giving each extract a title and the words and sentences which make an impact – something they need to think about in their own writing. They are given further support by examining the features of effective personal narrative while being reminded that, with this kind of writing, we cannot be prescriptive about structure and style (see Figure 5).

A further stage promoted in the 'sequence for teaching writing' is that of demonstrating how to write a particular kind of text. The teacher models the process of translating thoughts into words on the page. In the role of writer, the teacher drafts opening sentences on the board, thinking aloud about word choices and sentence construction, editing and redrafting. Pupils see an expert practitioner at work and witness the thoughtful, chaotic, creative process that writing can be. They can then try this out in their own work.

'Writing floats on a sea of talk' observes James Britton (1969) and all learners, bilingual learners in particular, need opportunities to share and explore ideas through structured listening and speaking activities. In this way, language is understood, practised, developed. In the work on 'Autobiography', we teachers shared key moments and experiences in our own lives, starting with the words 'I'll never forget the time when ...' We then invited questions and comments from the pupils. The process of planning and teaching in partnership can make the experience of engaging in dialogue with pupils easier to manage and sustain. Once teachers are actively reflecting on their practice and perhaps taking more risks in

	Extract number 4	Extract number 5	Extract number 6
1. Who do you think wrote this? (Man/woman? Age? Nationality). What clues have you found in the text about the writer?	This was write by his Daughter, when she had grown up. We think shes English or American.	This was write by Nelson mandela hes was about os when he wrote it (4 year ago). Hes is agrican president now.	We think it is a man who write this. I think hes about 60 – 70
2. When do you think this was written? (Recently? 20/50/100 years ago?) Give reasons for your answer	we think it was written 20-40 years ago.	This was write 4 years ago.	We think this was write about 15 - 30 years ago
3. What are the main things that the writer is saying and how does he or she feel?	we think her father die & she wanted him to see when she was growen up, We think she is sad about it to	~~There.~~ ~~Shouted~~ Asrica Should be gree 8or all race & get all people equacall.	he says about how peacesul it is.
4. What do you feel when you read this extract? Which words or phrases do you think are most powerful?	our group thinks it's a sad · poem. The powersul words are, He would have grown to admire the women I becom	we seel everyone should get along. the chains on all os my people where chains on me.	We seel carm & gentle
5. What title would you give it?	The memory os my dad	Freedom os my people	~~A Intent Poem~~ I'am listening to Istanbun, intent, my eyes closed.

Figure 4

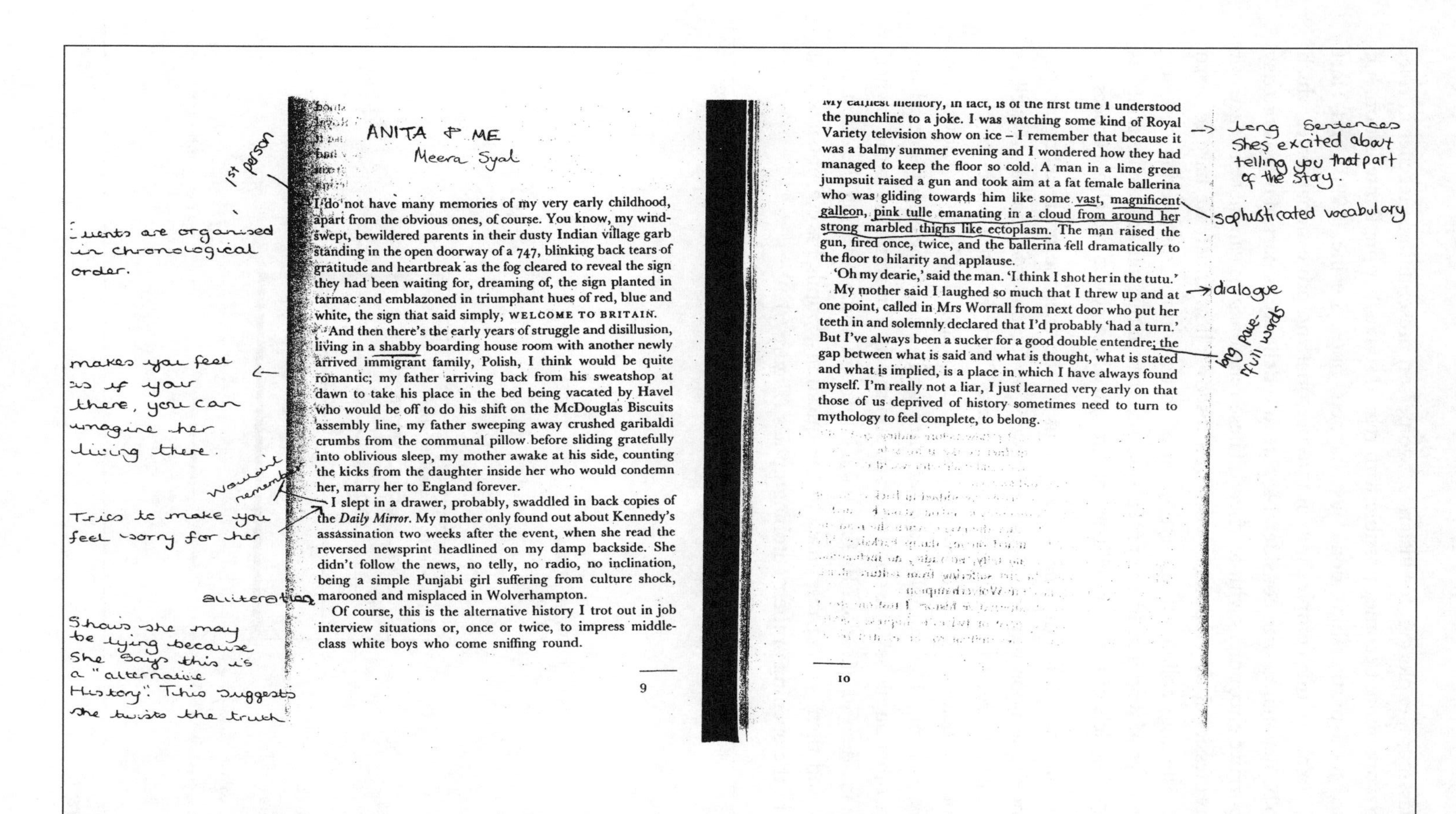

ANITA & ME
Meera Syal

I do not have many memories of my very early childhood, apart from the obvious ones, of course. You know, my wind-swept, bewildered parents in their dusty Indian village garb standing in the open doorway of a 747, blinking back tears of gratitude and heartbreak as the fog cleared to reveal the sign they had been waiting for, dreaming of, the sign planted in tarmac and emblazoned in triumphant hues of red, blue and white, the sign that said simply, WELCOME TO BRITAIN.

And then there's the early years of struggle and disillusion, living in a shabby boarding house room with another newly arrived immigrant family, Polish, I think would be quite romantic; my father arriving back from his sweatshop at dawn to take his place in the bed being vacated by Havel who would be off to do his shift on the McDouglas Biscuits assembly line, my father sweeping away crushed garibaldi crumbs from the communal pillow before sliding gratefully into oblivious sleep, my mother awake at his side, counting the kicks from the daughter inside her who would condemn her, marry her to England forever.

I slept in a drawer, probably, swaddled in back copies of the *Daily Mirror*. My mother only found out about Kennedy's assassination two weeks after the event, when she read the reversed newsprint headlined on my damp backside. She didn't follow the news, no telly, no radio, no inclination, being a simple Punjabi girl suffering from culture shock, marooned and misplaced in Wolverhampton.

Of course, this is the alternative history I trot out in job interview situations or, once or twice, to impress middle-class white boys who come sniffing round.

9

My earliest memory, in fact, is of the first time I understood the punchline to a joke. I was watching some kind of Royal Variety television show on ice – I remember that because it was a balmy summer evening and I wondered how they had managed to keep the floor so cold. A man in a lime green jumpsuit raised a gun and took aim at a fat female ballerina who was gliding towards him like some vast, magnificent galleon, pink tulle emanating in a cloud from around her strong marbled thighs like ectoplasm. The man raised the gun, fired once, twice, and the ballerina fell dramatically to the floor to hilarity and applause.

'Oh my dearie,' said the man. 'I think I shot her in the tutu.'

My mother said I laughed so much that I threw up and at one point, called in Mrs Worrall from next door who put her teeth in and solemnly declared that I'd probably 'had a turn.' But I've always been a sucker for a good double entendre; the gap between what is said and what is thought, what is stated and what is implied, is a place in which I have always found myself. I'm really not a liar, I just learned very early on that those of us deprived of history sometimes need to turn to mythology to feel complete, to belong.

10

Figure 5

the classroom, exploring, for instance, two person presentations, teacher in role, group work, more becomes possible with regard to teacher/pupil interaction. 'Of course, good partnerships don't just happen' notes Levine (1990) and Hart (1991) explores the 'complex web of interpersonal and professional issues which has to be negotiated with considerable care and delicacy as part of our day to day collaborative encounters with teachers'. These relationships can make us face our own professional development needs and discover how much we have to learn about listening, collaborating, letting go of some control, discovering new and better ways of working. In the process we see that pupils gain too witnessing, as they do, models of professional partnerships in which adults are also learners.

Pupils consider different types of questions in the exercise on recalling an experience, questions requiring yes/no answers or factual information as well as those eliciting reflective, evaluative responses. Then they are ready to choose memorable incidents of their own to discuss in groups. The activity shown here invites each pupil to complete the sentence and to pass the sheet around the group; other pupils ask one question each and the sheet is returned to the 'owner' of the incident in question. By first talking through and answering the questions orally and then writing responses to the questions, pupils have a possible first draft to the opening of their autobiographies (Figure 6).

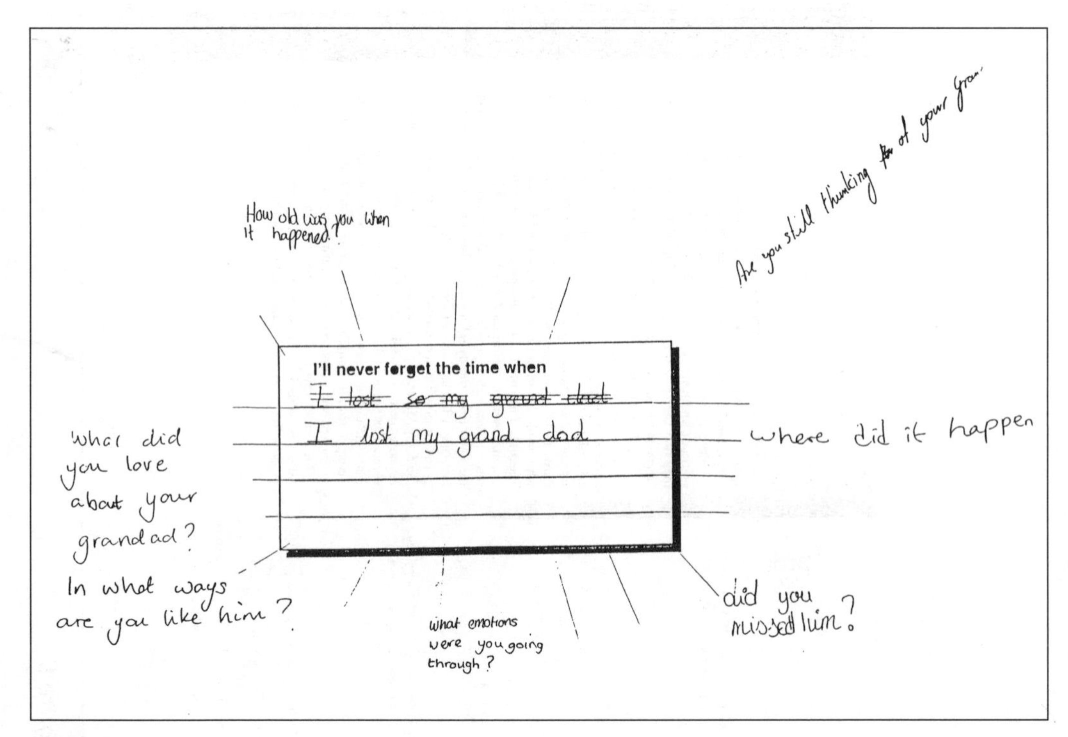

Figure 6

Talk was the starting point too in the work on *Romeo and Juliet.* Pupils unpack a story sack, a small wooden chest containing key elements or props from the story: an invitation to a ball, a mask, a wedding ring, a phial of liquid. They use the objects to tell stories of their own creation before hearing Shakespeare's plot. Once the text has been 'warmed up' in this way (Meek, 1991), pupils are ready to study the play by actively reading key extracts (in translation where necessary/possible), watching video versions, taking part in drama activities and discussing themes and issues through structured talk exercises. They can express their understanding in a variety of ways – a fortune line is a good starting point or revision exercise, as it requires an overview of the play as well as a character's journey through it. The chapter on fortune lines in *Probing Understanding* by White and Gunstone (1992) offers guidance on the use of this technique in the classroom. Some pupils, including those newly arrived, may be given the significant moments to plot; others will decide on and write the key experiences themselves (see Figure 7).

Working in partnership in multilingual classrooms, we have used our combined knowledge of language acquisition and effective learning to plan for structured, interactive lessons. The work of Wray and Lewis (1997)) enabled us to develop our approaches further. The EXIT model, in particular, informed our thinking and we drew on this in the way we planned – thinking first of the objective or outcome to be achieved and then designing the steps to get there (see Figure 8).

This way of working has been effective when planning for all learners, starting, as it does, with the expectation that every pupil can meet the objective given the appropriate scaffold, support and challenge.

In another Year 9 class, pupils are required to imitate a distinctive narrative voice, that of serial killer Shelter in Robert Swindell's novel *Stone Cold* (1997). Blanche who, like Chlève, is from the Democratic Republic of Congo and who speaks Lingala and French, in which she is highly literate, writes as Shelter. Shelter poses as a do-gooder and entices young, homeless victims to his flat with the offer of food and a bath. Blanche's reference to Shelter's 'army' is to the bodies accumulating in the basement of the flat (see Figure 9).

Blanche has been successful as a writer in various ways. She has

- used appropriate vocabulary that reflects the character's military background
- handled the material skilfully, conveying the contrast between Shelter's assumed persona and his real thoughts and intentions
- conveyed Shelter's pride in his own cunning and his skills as a killer

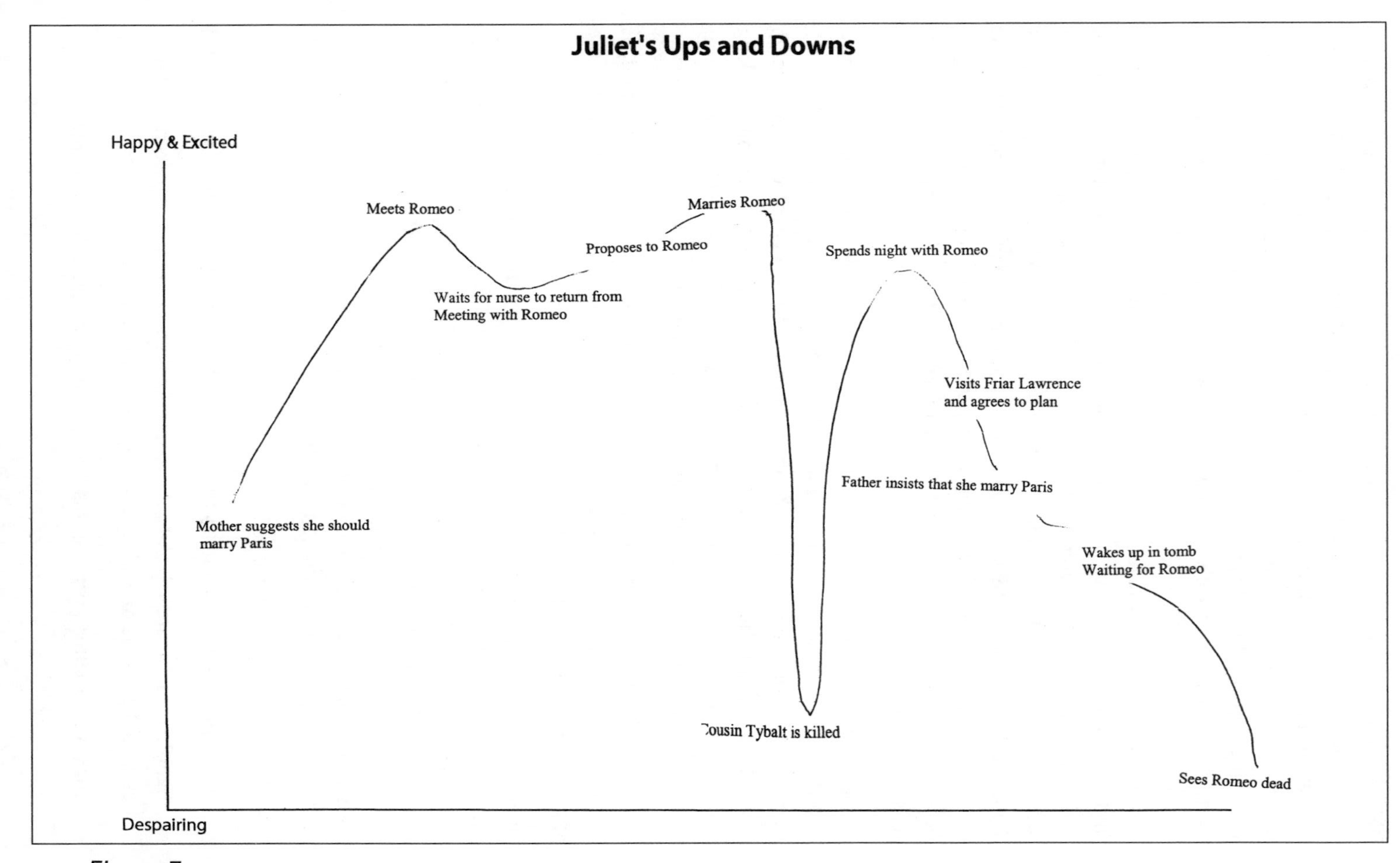
Juliet's Ups and Downs
Happy & Excited
Despairing
Mother suggests she should marry Paris
Meets Romeo
Waits for nurse to return from Meeting with Romeo
Proposes to Romeo
Marries Romeo
Cousin Tybalt is killed
Spends night with Romeo
Visits Friar Lawrence and agrees to plan
Father insists that she marry Paris
Wakes up in tomb Waiting for Romeo
Sees Romeo dead

Figure 7

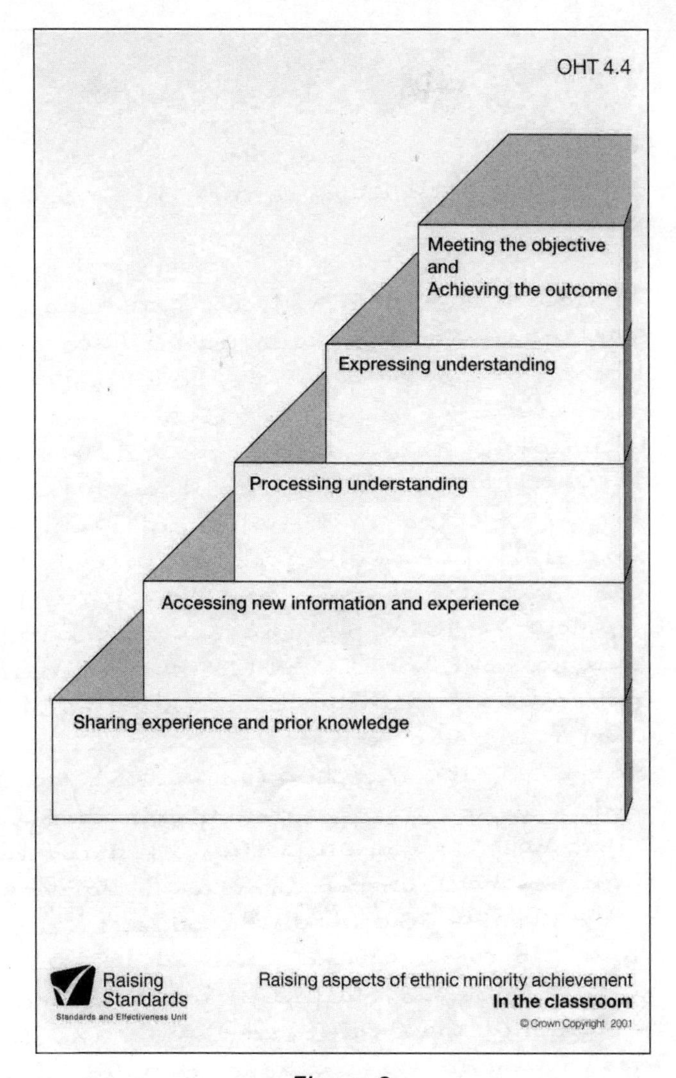
OHT 4.4
Meeting the objective
and
Achieving the outcome
Expressing understanding
Processing understanding
Accessing new information and experience
Sharing experience and prior knowledge
Raising
Standards
Standards and Effectiveness Unit
Raising aspects of ethnic minority achievement
In the classroom
© Crown Copyright 2001

Figure 8

6.6.03.

Daily Routine orders 17.

As you know my mission is to clean up the street of London; it was about 22.00 hours when I began my nightly patrol, I had spotted him and there he ~~was~~ is now, he came to me like a little cat who wants his milk. This one is so shy and I think he'll be better in the army. It was not that hard as I thought Poor sod I thought, so innocent, thinks he has another chance at life. little lad, did he know he has no chance at all.
"You alright son?" I asked him like I was concerned. "yeah I'm fine Grand dad, he replied What's up big belly.
Nothing. It's just seem be lost my lad" I said; by now I was really pissed off.
Is that how you always sleep? I asked him
yeah so what's wrong with you? Nothing I said he was to rude and I couldn't bother to keep talking.
I asked to come around, without saying anything he just dropp his stuff and followed me.
He now tried to be nice and thanks me so he said ~~goes~~, I can do the washing everyday if you want me to. I didn't say anything but I knew he ~~s~~ won't do it, by golly he won't ha ha hay!

An excellent effort, Blanche. You have really captured Shelter's "voice". Keep up the good work.

Figure 9

- understood and subtly conveyed the nature of the character. For example, the lack of respect from the young victim implied in 'big belly' is exactly the sort of behaviour that Shelter uses to justify his crimes.

The challenge for Blanche was considerable, but the work undertaken in class leading up to this writing shows the scaffolding and support that enabled her to achieve success.

Firstly, the mixed ability class read the novel over two weeks, including in homework time. They did so in a mixture of whole class and group sessions. Blanche and another French-speaking, newly arrived pupil had three sessions with a native French-speaking support teacher. The deployment of a member of the Modern Foreign Languages department in a support role was arranged at the beginning of the school year in response to the arrival of a number of French-speaking pupils in the school. The support teacher was able to summarise the story and look in detail at key passages. This allowed Blanche to enjoy the story and enter into the excitement of the unfolding narrative. At other times the work with the support teacher took Blanche a little ahead of the rest of the class, placing her in something of an 'expert' role in the class session that followed. It was in one of these lessons that Blanche made her first unprompted contribution to whole class discussion and received a round of applause. All teachers will recognise what an important breakthrough that can be for the newcomer who is learning English.

Secondly, on completion of the novel, several passages in Shelter's voice were carefully examined. Following a starter activity matching examples of Shelter's characteristically 'military' lexical range, pupils worked in small groups to locate other examples of his style. A new scenario was suggested for another murder by

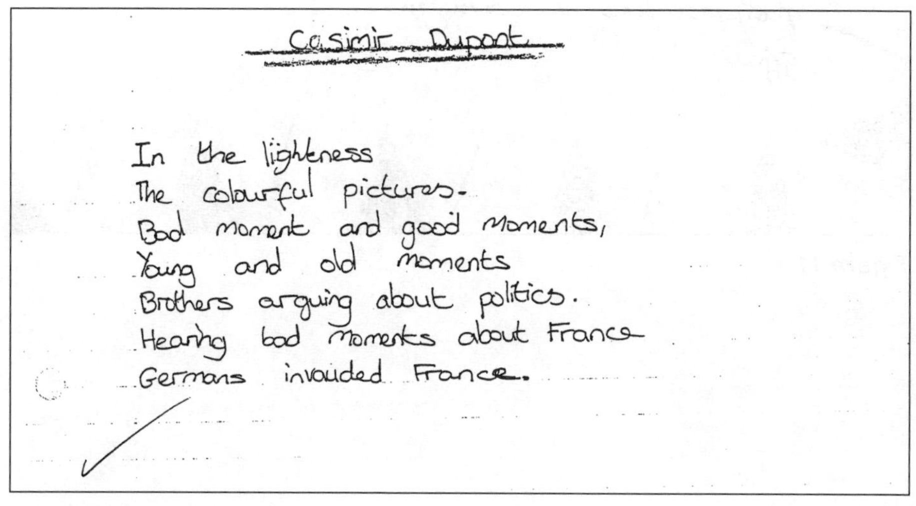

Casimir Dupont

In the lightness
The colourful pictures.
Bad moment and good Moments,
Young and old moments
Brothers arguing about politics.
Hearing bad moments about France
Germans invauded France.

Figure 10

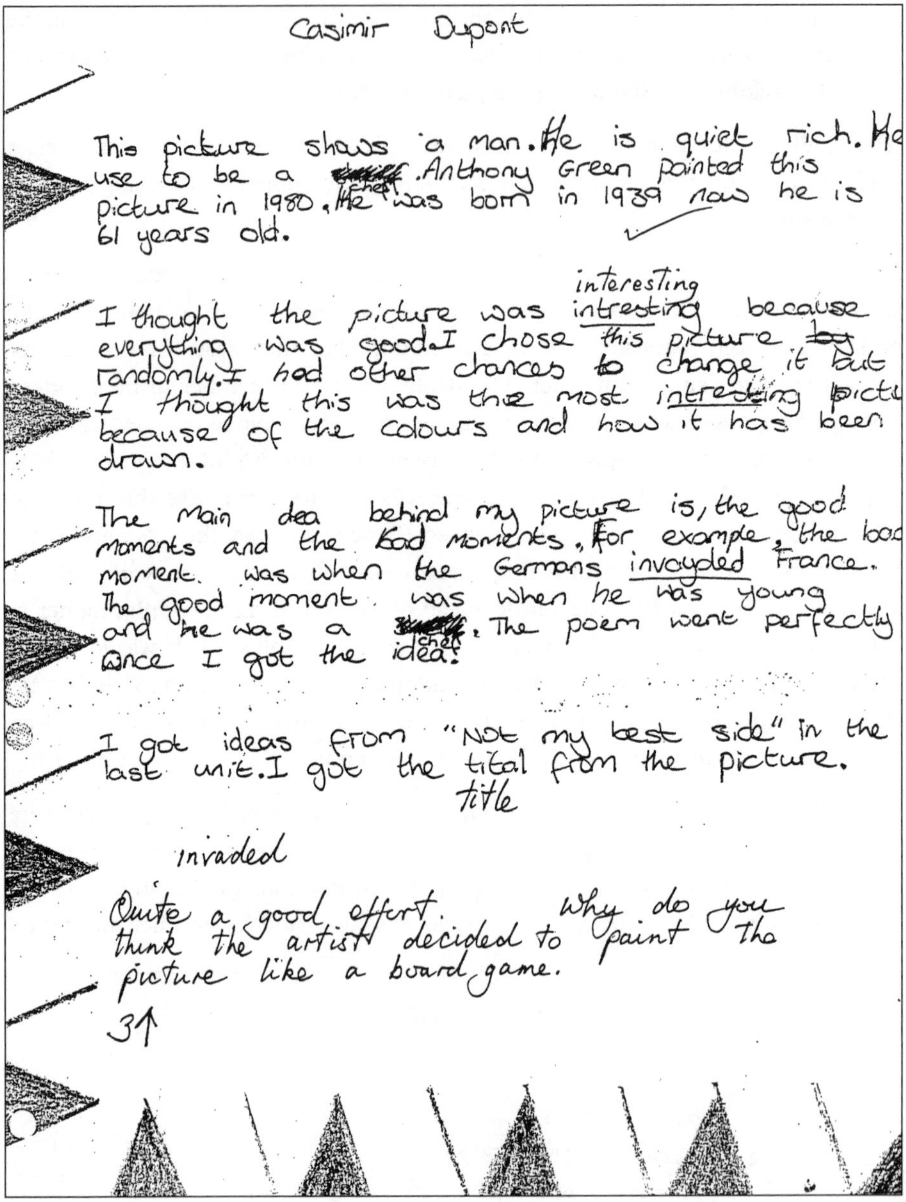

Casimir Dupont

This picture shows a man. He is quiet rich. He use to be a ~~chief~~ chef. Anthony Green painted this picture in 1980. He was born in 1939 now he is 61 years old.

I thought the picture was intresting (interesting) because everything was good. I chose this picture ~~by~~ randomly. I had other chances to change it but I thought this was the most intresting pictu because of the colours and how it has been drawn.

The Main dea behind my picture is, the good moments and the bad moments. For example, the bad moment was when the Germans invayded France. The good moment was when he was young and he was a ~~chief~~ chef. The poem went perfectly once I got the idea!

I got ideas from "Not my best side" in the last unit. I got the tital from the picture.
title

invaded

Quite a good effort. Why do you think the artist decided to paint the picture like a board game.
3↑

Figure 11

Shelter and the class were invited to try retelling the story of this murder in Shelter's voice.

For this second stage in the work the support teacher was only present for a short time. Joint planning between the English teacher and support teacher ensured that Blanche gained maximum benefit from limited support time. As in the examples described earlier, good planning and lesson design improves learning for all members of the class. If the teacher unpicks the learning process for the benefit of pupils learning English as an additional language, *all* students will benefit.

Blanche was literate in her first language and highly motivated. Suleyman, a Turkish speaking year 8 boy, was barely literate in Turkish, disaffected and already earning a reputation for being difficult. Nonetheless he was able, with the appropriate level of support and challenge, to produce his first sustained piece of writing since arriving in Year 7.

The unit of work 'Pictures and Poems' had been devised by members of the English and Art department and an EAL support teacher. The teachers felt the pictures would facilitate access for all, and careful scaffolding would build in appropriate levels of challenge for all.

Suleyman's piece was the culmination of a sequence of lessons. In art lessons students produced an image based on a poem. In English they experimented with various poetic forms using pictures as stimuli. The final activity in English was to write a poem about a picture *and* a commentary on their own writing. Sets of A4 art cards were used and each student chose one of these to interpret. The art cards had some information about the artist and the picture, and students were invited to make use of this in their work. Central to the unit was teacher modelling of the writing process, drafting thoughts and ideas on a whiteboard or OHP and talking about structure and language choices. Before the students began the final task, the teacher presented her own poem and a commentary that explained how she had interpreted and described the image. Suleyman's poem and commentary are shown in Figures 10 and 11 on pages 41 and 42.

This was not a major achievement in itself. Much more impressive was Suleyman's willingness to present both picture and poem to the class and describe his reactions to the picture and what he wanted to say about it in his poem. What moved Suleyman forward in this unit was his level of engagement. He began to take himself seriously as a learner. For many recently arrived students with little experience of schooling and, more crucially, no experience of success in the classroom, this can be a breakthrough.

Once again, the planning of this work, the process of teacher modelling, and the time taken to find stimulating and engaging materials paid off. And not just for Suleyman, but for the whole class. The most able writers produced poems that were crafted and polished and commentaries that described a real involvement in the writing process. The level of involvement came not just from the quality of the materials but from the purposeful atmosphere promoted by the teacher demonstrating the way in which pupils could share and discuss their work with one another.

The examples shown in this chapter illustrate how effective learning is supported by good teaching. And the learning is achieved by all the pupils. Good teaching is by its nature inclusive, because it is based on a knowledge of pupils and an understanding of the learning process. Teachers need to be able to unravel the way in which pupils learn and reassemble this process to provide access and the greatest chance of success for all.

3

FLUENT MATHS

Vasant Mahandru

An elephant is about 5.67 metres high and its baby is 3.38 metres high. How much metres are they altogether?

This was the question posed by a bilingual pupil when asked to suggest a context for the mathematical operation: 5.67 m + 3.38 m =

Her response illustrates some of the issues that affect how bilingual pupils learn mathematics. It would be wrong to generalise, but the language of maths can certainly present significant challenges – as well as opportunities – for acquiring vocabulary and genres to all pupils and especially to those learning English as an additional language. They arise both when these pupils are reading and making sense of questions and when they are writing to make the problem solving process explicit. Many pupils will understand the concepts involved but they may find it difficult to discern the mathematical problem embedded in a question or to communicate their comprehension in English. By using the word 'altogether', the pupil in the example above signalled that she knew the two numbers had to be added (and she has illustrated this graphically). Two other errors, however, show that while she has acquired the concept of addition, she has struggled to explain her understanding accurately:

she used 'about' before an exact figure of 5.67 m
she used 'how much' instead of 'how many'

She has still to learn that 'how much' is used for non-countable nouns whereas 'how many' is used for countable nouns.

Wide-ranging programmes to enhance the teaching and learning of mathematics for all pupils are currently being implemented at national, local and individual school level. The mathematics strand of the Key Stage 3 Strategy defines numeracy:

> It is more than an ability to do basic arithmetic. It involves developing confidence and competence with numbers and measures. It requires understanding the number system, a repertoire of mathematical techniques and an inclination and ability to solve quantitative or spatial problems in a range of contexts. Numeracy also demands understanding of the ways in which data are gathered by counting and measuring, and presented in graphs, diagrams, charts and tables. (*KS3 National Strategy Framework for teaching mathematics*, 2001)

The 'Thinking Maths' approach developed in the CAME (Cognitive Acceleration in Maths Education) project at Kings' College (1998) is similarly underpinned by the idea of challenging pupils to grasp key mathematical concepts. It offers important opportunities for pupils to think aloud the processes they are using to compute, estimate and deduce, an experience that is highly conducive to language development as well as academic learning. Many bilingual pupils come to school with mathematical concepts already embedded in their minds, together with strategies for calculating and problem solving. When these pupils encounter new methods and techniques, they learn that there are different ways of carrying out mathematical processes. They are then required to think about the respective merits and demerits of the methods and so enhance their understanding as well as their language acquisition.

The Key Stage 3 publication *Access and engagement in mathematics* (2002) offers useful guidance and interesting case studies of work in Camden, Enfield and Westminster schools.

Another project, run in a north London school, focuses on providing resources in pupils' first language and has proved popular with both pupils and parents. Annie Gammon in *Talking Maths Talking Languages* (1993) discusses the way in which bilingual pupils can be encouraged to develop mathematical understanding through using their first languages, and develop fluency in these languages while doing so.

Such projects and publications promote empowering approaches to the teaching and learning of mathematics. This chapter is more modest: it suggests ways in which teachers can, easily and with little extra preparation, make the language of maths more accessible to bilingual pupils, and it shows how the pupils can be supported to express themselves with greater mathematical fluency.

Most children start learning maths specific language in early childhood. Words like 'share' 'add', 'take away' are part of a child's vocabulary and most children know the names of some shapes, like square and circle. Bilingual pupils acquiring maths terminology in English are learning a second – or additional – set of vocabulary. In the classroom it often takes the form of two phases of acquisition which are not necessarily sequential: from the first language into formal English and from formal terminology into informal expressions as used by teachers and peers in the classroom.

The experience of one Turkish speaking pupil learning maths illustrates the process. When she was learning maths vocabulary, she was taught the word 'multiply' for the process she knew in Turkish as *çarpmark*. But she was puzzled when the maths teacher used the word 'times'. Now she had to make another transition – from 'multiply' to 'times' – to follow what was going on in the classroom. Similarly she learns 'subtract' as an English word for the Turkish *çikarmak* and then has to substitute it for 'take away'.

Neither is it enough for pupils to learn key subject specific words and their definitions in English; they need to know that the meaning of words changes according to context. A Bengali speaking pupil was confused by the word 'square' and its forms. She understood it firstly as the name of a shape with equal sides at right angles to each other. She then had to learn that it could be used with numbers to mean something different.

2 squares ⟶ □□

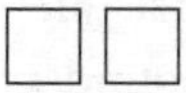

seems clear but

2 cm squares ⟶ ?

Does it mean 2 squares of 1 cm side?

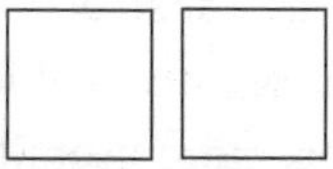

1cm 1cm

Or does it mean squares – we don't how many – of 2 cm side each?

2 cm 2 cm 2 cm

To complicate matters further, the following has another meaning

2 squared ⟶ 2^2

Similarly, the words for numbers can be confusing for bilingual learners who are still acquiring fluency in English. When a teacher read out a question to the class, requiring them to work out how much it would cost to stay in a hotel for thirteen nights, one pupil thought she had heard thirty nights – a mistake easily made. All 'teen' numbers can present a problem to pupils who are learning to distinguish certain sounds – in this case 'teen' and 'ty' as unstressed syllables at the end of the number.

A similar difficulty can arise over the English ending of the ordinal form of numbers in '...rd' and '...th' for the denominators in a fraction. 'One third' 1/3, 'four sevenths' 4/7 and 'three twentieths' 3/20 can be puzzling. Many languages do not have such a form for numbers. For example, in Turkish, the fraction 1/10 is expressed in a way that translates into English as 'one divided by ten'. Consequently, if someone says: 'he won the race by three hundredths of a second', it might sound like three hundred seconds to someone unfamiliar with this way of expressing a fraction.

The way questions are structured can also be a challenge. An analysis of questions shows that maths problems consist of two parts: the statement and the question. Sometimes the two are fused together. Take the following examples

> A tin of baked beans costs 35p. How much will 5 tins cost?
> Find the cost of 7 packets of biscuits costing 48 p each.

A bilingual pupil will probably find the first question easier because it is neatly split into statement and question and the boundary is clearly marked. The second problem, written in the imperative, is more complex since the statement is embedded in the question.

Mathematical problems and instructions need to be either structured in such a way that they become more accessible to pupils who are developing linguistic competence in English or, more usefully, pupils need to learn to extract the statement and the question from the rubric of the problem. It also helps the pupils if words are used that can act as triggers to the mathematical operation they are required to tackle. Consider the following problem solving example of a question:

> Five friends go to a restaurant for a meal. The charges are £15 per head. How much will they have to pay?

The question seems straightforward but you couldn't fault the pupils if they answered: 'They have to pay £15 per head'. What is required here is the total amount that will have to be paid: 15 x 5 = £75. Inserting 'altogether' into the question would make it far clearer: 'How much will they have to pay *altogether*?'

Similarly, using 'each' in a question will signal to pupils that they need to use division. 'A bag contains 36 sweets. Four children share them equally amongst themselves. How many does each child get?'

There are a number of such trigger words – all, every, either, neither – that can support children in identifying which operation they need to perform. They make the implicit operations explicit for bilingual pupils.

Developing children's mathematical language should not be confined to equipping them with a full repertoire of subject specific vocabulary and knowledge of the structure of questions. They require fluency of expression based on quick responses to short questions as well as statements. A maths lesson which supports bilingual pupils needs to contain a significant element of oracy: a regular slot where pupils ask and answer oral questions.

As recommended by the Key Stage 3 National Strategy, most schools have three-part maths lessons with a starter to warm up and stimulate the pupils' numeracy skills. Bilingual pupils whose language needs are developing can benefit enormously from the starter sessions, particularly if teachers use visual and tactile resources such as white boards and number sticks.

The Key Stage 3 Strategy recommends 'oral and mental starters to develop pupils' mental agility and their visualisation, thinking and communication skills'. One of the activities is called a 'loop' card or 'follow me' activity. All the pupils are given cards bearing a question and an answer. One pupil asks the question on her card and the pupil who has the right answer gives the answer and then asks his question. Year 7 classes use an oral starter which involves a task aimed at enabling all the pupils to calculate the passage of time. Each pupil has a card with a 24 hour clock time and + or – a number of minutes. Pupils have to frame their own statements and questions.

Card 1	Card 2
..............(statement)	............(statement)
19-15	20-05
..............(question)	............(question)
+ 50 minutes	-15 minutes

The pupil with the first card says:

The time now is 19-15. What will be the time in 50 minutes?

The pupil with the second card says:

The time now is 20-05. What was the time 15 minutes ago?

The question and answer session helps pupils develop their language as well as their numeracy skills, particularly if teachers or teaching assistants are giving feedback on the language use and rewording or scribing it where this is helpful.

To help develop their comprehension of written questions, pupils can be required to invent their own questions which they then ask partners to solve. This reinforces mathematical concepts; pupils are required to think through ways of checking their understanding of particular ideas and operations. It also helps to develop maths specific vocabulary.

A number of variations can be used to give pupils practice in this field. The first is simply to give a number operation and ask pupils to write a question about it (as illustrated at the start of this chapter). For example, Year 7 pupils were given the following calculation:

50 kg – 12.5 kg

One bilingual pupil wrote: 'There is a bag of 50 kg of flour in a bakery. They used 12.5 kg from the big bag. How much kgs of flour is left in the bag?'

In response to the calculation 75cm -18cm, another pupil wrote:

> There were a number of teachers in school who were 75cm tall. All of them teachers left and there were only teachers that were 18cm tall. How much has the tallness gone down by?

This pupil understands the notion of subtraction but needs to make concrete her knowledge of units of measurement – and to recognise the somewhat surreal scenario she depicts here! She also needs guidance on the use of pronouns when writing standard English ('them teachers') and on nouns relating to size ('height' rather than 'tallness').

In another activity the teacher says simply:

'The answer is ... What is the question?' For example: 'The answer is 48 square metres. What is the question?' 'A room is 8 metres long and 6 metres wide. What is the area of the room?' is one possible answer.

Devising supplementary questions provides an opportunity for pupils to extend their knowledge and understanding e.g. 'How much would it cost to carpet this room if carpet costs £... per square metre?'

Developing mathematical concepts through the medium of a new or additional language is made easier if the lessons are supported by visual and tactile resources. Spatial maths would be almost impossible to teach without visual illustrations, and topics like fractions, percentages or averages become more real if actual pictures or artefacts are used. In a lesson on mean, mode and median, the textbook had questions about pupils' heights and weights etc. To make it real, pupils were asked the following question:

> How many pens does each one of you have?

The whole lesson was based on determining the average pens per pupil in the class and whether the boys or the girls had most. This made it interesting and accessible to the pupils.

In addition to ensuring that maths is relevant to pupils' own experiences, teachers can actively extend awareness and challenge stereotyping:

> Anti-racist mathematics teaching ... must mean at minimum: deliberately seeking out knowledge of the Third World peoples and making it easily accessible to all children learning mathematics. (Shan and Bailey, 1994)

In a unit of work on data handling, one maths department used weather data from Bangladesh to engage Bangladeshi pupils. And in a class which included Turkish pupils, the population of Turkey was similarly used to construct a population pyramid in analysing patterns of age ranges. The use of appropriate content in all sorts of mathematical problems can engage the pupils in the subject.

Numeracy across the curriculum supports bilingual pupils, along with their monolingual peers, to acquire mathematical skills in context. A Year 8 Geography lesson addresses temperature in different parts of the world and this topic is developed in maths and science. Pupils are given a list of big cities in the world with their temperatures and hours of sunshine and asked to work out the correlation between the temperature and hours of sunshine. Again, the cities chosen are from the countries familiar to the pupils.

The underlying context for all the approaches outlined in this chapter is the dynamic learning environment, one in which the teacher knows each pupil and values and includes their languages and experiences. In such environments, learning becomes relevant, active and collaborative. Pupils are supported and challenged; they make progress both as mathematicians and as linguists.

4

ROMA ASYLUM SEEKERS: THE DOUBLE WHAMMY

Graham Went

I am one of a group of Year 7s and it's my first day at secondary school. It is a Monday morning in early September, and we're huddled in a corner of a vast tarmac 'play' ground, watching as huge people from higher up the school hurtle around. They appear to rule by volume, size and number. The roughness of their play is alarming, and to venture further than this corner will surely invite serious injury. Other calmer activities are going on too but we don't take these in. My little huddle contains all the failed 11 plusers from our primary school ('failures' before we've even started). I feel physically sick. Do they really stuff your head down the toilet? Still, I can count my blessings. Home is just around the corner, I have lived in this area all my life and know dozens of people here. I have older friends at the school and I have friends in the same boat. Oh how we empathise with each other – not that we used such words! We go inside. The place is huge – but at least I can speak and understand the lingo and read the notices. The teachers seem friendly. I suppose I'll make out.

Five years later, I'm head boy – so I guess I did...

We've all been there. We've all known exclusion to some degree. What are the factors that enabled us to overcome it – if we did? What tipped the balance one way or the other?

Who is that in the corner of the playground? It's Roman from the Czech Republic, or Milan from Poland, or Danielle from Romania. I wonder how many blessings they're counting?

This chapter considers how the Roma fare on balance, and the issues this raises for schools. A number of bold statements highlight some of the factors that make a significant difference for Roma pupils. They head the presentations of good practice scenarios which have been drawn from case studies as well as ideal theoretical models, to promote discussion and inspire development work.

A good practice school empathises

As part of an inservice training programme, I try to develop an idea of what it must be like for a Roma child entering school in Britain, by drawing out themes from the school experiences of the group. Let me take you through it. It's worth taking time to pause and reflect on each question before reading on.

1. Jot down the most frightening experience of your school life.
2. Similarly, your most pleasurable experience.
3. When you recall your school days, do you remember them as a generally happy, positive experience, or would the opposite be true? Spend a few moments to tease out the reasons why.

I have found this a great way to start the session – especially if as a trainer I am prepared to be open and frank about some of my own experiences. Participants are on familiar territory and many will share their experiences. One person's story will spark another's; there is much amusement; much empathy. The problem comes when bringing this part to a conclusion and moving on. There have been times, however, when participants have been upset by things they have remembered, and although I have no desire to expose vulnerable sensitivities, the fact that these surface is highly significant in the light of what I am trying to draw out.

We move on.

4. How many changes of school did you have?

The evidence elicited from this question is that the more changes of school, the less likely that schooling will have been a positive experience

We then try to distil the factors that enable pupils to feel at ease and positive about their school experience. Four main factors appear to be significant: the pupils need to

- be confident about how the school works
- have an accepting group of friends within the school
- encounter staff who praise them for good work, who are understanding and reassuring
- have families that are comfortable with the system

A good practice school understands

The Roma are viewed by the UK as economic migrants, but few can offer skilled work. Consequently most asylum applications by East European Roma are unsuccessful. But those who are here face a double whammy. Newcomers to this country – especially those unable to speak English – have shakier foundations on which to build a successful school career than do children who were born here. But it is especially difficult for the Roma. They have obstacles to overcome over and above those encountered by other asylum seeker/refugee groups..

Language issues are not straightforward. I am sitting with an interpreter in the home of a Roma family. The conversation is very protracted. I speak and the interpreter interprets into the national language for the father, and he in turn interprets into Romanes for the benefit of the mother. Responses then take the reverse order. Several thoughts arise. Do the messages really get through? How accurately did mum receive what I said, and how accurately did I receive what mum had to say? How well is this interpreter being received by this family? After all, she represents the non-Roma national, from a country where racist hatred has spewed for centuries, and particularly since the fall of communism – that is why they are here. Then again, what are the interpreter's views of this Roma family. I don't think the quality of interpretation is in question or that nuances are deliberately inserted – but I don't know for certain.

Most of the Roma I've worked with are not literate in either their national language or Romanes. Our bureaucracy deals poorly with illiteracy. Some Roma parents had no experience of schooling, and for many of those who did it didn't last long. Few Czech and Slovak Roma who attended school in the 1970s and 1980s describe it as a purposeful learning experience. It normally meant being placed separately at the rear of the classroom and then ignored. School was feared because it had the authority to assign Roma students to a special school for mentally handicapped children (European Roma Rights Centre, 1999:22), or even move them to a prison-like institution. Romanian Roma children, on the other hand, frequently found themselves in racially segregated classes where they were treated as 'socially handicapped' or denied access to education altogether (European Roma Rights Centre, 2001:110-115). Most children of Roma asylum seekers from Latvia and Lithuania will have had no experience of education in their home countries (see Rutter, 2003).

Few Roma acknowledge that what they learnt in school is relevant to their lives. School experience is contrasted with the purposeful learning of a trade in a safe family setting. Positive accounts of education are more likely to refer to sympathetic teachers than to the academic merits of the school. For many Roma children in the 1990s schooling was obligatory and underlined exclusion. Although

Roma in Poland and former Czechoslovakia had no difficulty accessing education, they were made unwelcome in school. A typical Czech Roma experience of school would include routine bullying that went 'unnoticed' by teachers, attempts by non-Roma parents to separate their children from Roma children, and the fear of the child being certified as 'stupid' and sent to a special school. Polish accounts tell often of schooling for a Roma child ending abruptly after a gang attack by non-Roma pupils. So it is not surprising that education in this country is approached with some trepidation.

The Roma have few effective support structures outside of the family. A group of Polish nationals, for example, might be unwelcoming to Polish Roma, and pan Roma groups have difficulties spanning the distinctiveness of each Roma national group. Add to that the effects of dispersal, and you end up with many small pockets of different Roma groups.

If asylum seekers in general get a bad press, the treatment of the Roma is often grotesque. This feeds public attitudes. As I pull up to visit a family I find the man of the house outside, washing egg off of the front window. 'Many times this, many times this!' he says in a resigned tone that lends weight to his words. And there's the family who will not let their children out of their sight for fear – born of experience – that they will get beaten up.

They are an understandably suspicious of authority. I knock on the door of a house for the first time. I represent the council, somebody who is going to tell/order/demand something. The negative experience of generations is not easily dispelled.

Few of these families can offer skills that are needed in this country and they are seen as economic migrants. Nationally, few asylum applications are successful.

Early education: I am in the home of a family where the oldest child is not yet four. She bustles around happily with a battered toy vacuum cleaner as we talk via the interpreter, and warmth, love and concern for the child is evident in word and deed. An under fives worker is with me. Eventually we have to bite the bullet and say that the family need to fill in an application form for admission to reception class. The idea is anathema to the parents . 'Back home they don't go in until they are 7!'

Early marriage and childbirth: we are now visiting a school aged mother. She is just 14 and the baby is nearly 12 months old. We explain the importance and the legal requirement of schooling. This too is unacceptable. 'How can it be possible for me to look after my baby and go to school?' On another occasion I am told that the very young looking 13 year old sitting quietly before me is about to get married and will therefore not be going to school It is explained that this is the way within the culture. It is not uncommon to find cultural practice challenging the law of the land.

A good practice school is informed and **knows about the language and history of Roma**

Unlike many refugee groups in the UK, Roma are not a homogeneous entity in terms of political affiliation, religion, nationality or even language. They are disparate and come from practically every Eastern European state. The factors that triggered this exodus are rooted in the exclusion of Roma in the redistribution of wealth, land and social roles following the political changes across the region between 1989 and 1999. No matter whether this change involved a full-scale war for independence as in Kosova, or 'velvet' privatisation as in the Czech Republic, racially motivated violence, marginalisation and expulsion of Roma accompanied it.

Since the early 1990s, Roma communities in Eastern Europe have been subject to numerous pogroms and attacks. In the Czech Republic, Slovakia and Romania, incitement of anti-Roma hatred has become a common tool by which to manipulate the electorate. Roma were portrayed as inherently criminal, underdeveloped and incapable of social integration. This hatred towards Roma was reinforced by racist media reports. Unsurprisingly, the polls across Eastern Europe in the 1990s revealed that 78 per cent of the respondents had negative attitudes to Roma (Demetr *et al*, 2000:229).

The social exclusion of Roma in the region has been characterised by inadequate access to employment, housing and education. They were the first to lose their jobs when the Communist policies of full employment in the early 1990s were dropped. By the mid nineties the rate of unemployment among Roma was 76 per cent in Bulgaria (Demetr *et al*, 2000:230), 70 per cent in the Czech Republic (European Roma Rights Centre, 1999:10) and 65 per cent in Romania (European Roma Rights Centre, 2001:97), with the overall unemployment rate in the same countries registering from five to fourteen times lower. Roma are more likely to live in substandard accommodation and there has been a regular pattern of forced evictions of Roma families or the bulldozing of entire shanty settlements in Romania.

Although these patterns of exclusion and violence represent a crisis stage in the history of Roma in Europe, they are far from new. From the early 16th century, Roma were for over two hundred years continually banished from one country to another. These expulsions started against the background of the general economic change triggered by the inflow of plundered gold from the newly discovered Americas and the consequent anti-vagrant laws that replaced the earlier tolerance of itinerants (Demetr *et al*, 2000:31). This often meant the death penalty or maiming for 'overstay' or 're-entry'. As non-citizens almost everywhere in Western Europe, Roma were not protected by the law and were subject to scapegoating and mob violence. Forced into the margins of host societies or hiding in woods, they were denied access to agriculture, normal business and any form of education. This persecution reinforced the itinerant factor in Roma cultures and some Roma opted for alternative survival strategies such as petty crime and begging. However, it was racism and not anti-nomadic sentiment that was at the core of the exclusionary practices against Roma in post-mediaeval Europe. Roma were dark-skinned, and for white Europeans this denoted evil, provoking wild myths about Roma. They were often treated as inferior and even subhuman, and there are accounts that eighteenth-century German aristocrats literally hunted them as wild animals. The same pattern of dehumanisation is found in Romania, where Roma were slaves, and the legislation of the country, in force until the mid 19th century, treated Roma as objects. These historical patterns reached the ultimate extreme in the Nazi attempt to exterminate them totally. Almost 500.000 Roma were killed (see Supple, 1999).

A good practice school makes a bold statement

Although still far from ideal, race relations in the UK have come a long way since Empire Windrush days. There have been changes of practice, in society in general and education in particular, which reflect a much healthier attitude to issues of race and culture. But we are selective, for whenever the conversation turns to Travellers or Gypsies or Roma it becomes evident that these groups are seldom included in the thinking. And in local or national papers we find reporting that would provoke national uproar if it involved any other group of people.

An equal opportunities statement is failing if it doesn't reflect an all-inclusive mindset, so what should the good practice school do? It would be impossible, even were it desirable, to list all ethnic groups in an attempt not to leave any out. Enfield LEA's pupil ethnic monitoring form has over 60 categories of ethnicity – and there are still several 'other' categories. Conversely, generalisations often don't push thinking to an all-inclusive boundary.

There are, however, good reasons for specifically mentioning Roma (and other Traveller groups) in documentation. There are two reasons for this. Firstly there is a need to counter the popular misunderstanding that these are people who have simply made a lifestyle choice. This assumption is what has placed these groups outside the remit. Secondly, making specific reference to Gypsy groups will challenge people to think beyond their limited multiethnic boxes. Good all-inclusive statements are a fundamental marker of a good practice school and are relevant for every school. Sadly, I still hear comments such as 'It isn't an issue for us – we don't have any of them'.

A good practice school ensures an inclusive curriculum

Having made a bold statement, a good practice school will want to see curriculum inclusion. Its staff will be building up a knowledge base of relevant cultures, and then transferring this to the curriculum. There isn't much curriculum material at present that provides ready made lessons – which creates difficulties for busy teachers – but there are untapped riches that should not be ignored. Many authorities have Refugee, Ethnic Minority and Traveller education teams that should be able to help.

Here are a few cameos of what has been – or could be – done.

- A group of children in a music lesson are listening to the famous Gypsy jazz guitarist, Django Reinhardt. The lesson is part of a broad programme of musical styles; each set within their social origins. Other strands will include Hungarian and Romanian folk music – both of which have been strongly influenced by itinerant Gypsy musicians. There will be Flamenco and music by Liszt and Brahms, both of whom were influenced by the power and vitality of Gypsy music.

- At another school a local family of Polish Roma musicians has been invited in to play. One of the children at the school has been playing an accordion. There isn't a note of music to be seen. Someone is taking photographs, which will be added to a wall display that has been started, using a commercially available picture set of Roma musicians. The children have been engrossed, and the Roma children in the school suddenly find a heightened level of acceptance. The Roma family have offered the class the use of a family video taken at a wedding where there is much music and dancing, and the teacher wonders if it would possible to arrange for a group of dancers to come in.

- Linked to this, the RE department might include a strand on a Roma wedding. There is considerable material here, not only in the wedding ceremony itself, but also in a study of Roma views and practice concerning marriage.

- Another group is looking at Roma poetry and literature. From this material the teacher skilfully draws out a range of thoughts and responses. She is using a set of poems included in a booklet produced by Camden Traveller Education Service in 1999. Simply by reading the titles, a skilled teacher will see potential... 'Ode to the Twentieth Century'... 'The Raid'... 'Only Ashes Remain'... 'White snows fall on Belarus'

- A younger group is studying houses and homes. Yes, there has been work on flats, semis and terraced houses, but this teacher has pushed out the boundaries. Caravan and cave dwellers have been considered, as well as accommodation in shanty towns, ghettos, gypsy encampments and forced settlements. Also featured is the experience of Ilona Lackova, a Gypsy woman in Slovakia who lives in a Gypsy settlement on the margins of mainstream society. The teacher has worked hard to tease out the reasons why people live as they do – and show how often it has little to do with personal choice.

- In a PHSE lesson pupils are studying bias in the media, using copies of articles and headlines in national and local papers. Part of the study looks at Roma coming to the UK, how they are being treated, and the issues around refugees trying to gt into the UK from the Sandgatte Migrant Centre in France, close to the Channel Tunnel entrance – and closed in 2002. The teacher is venturing boldly here. He is digging at the roots of racism: there are pupils who will be quite happy to regurgitate the negative – what they have read, seen and heard. This is racism awareness work where the responses clearly indicate the need for the bold statement advocated earlier.
- Another teacher is using a modified version of the inservice training I give to professionals. Pupils are very ready to express their feelings and the teacher expertly steers thinking towards what the isolated newcomer might be experiencing. The lesson is set in a wider context of being a refugee, but the Roma experience is prominently featured. There is some brilliant role-play between 'Refugee' and 'Home Office official'. The teacher asks how desperate must you be to come into the country clinging underneath a train or hiding in the back of a lorry.
- A history lesson looks at the rise of the neo nazi movement since the demise of communism in Eastern Europe, and illustrates this with examples of racist attacks on the Roma.
- A sixth form group is studying the Holocaust. They are considering the evil thinking that underpinned the systematic slaughter of Jews, but they are also using the excellent material produced by Kent Traveller Education Service which gives information about the tens of thousands of European Roma who perished in the death camps. They have been reading extracts from the novel *And the Violins Stopped Playing* by Alexander Ramati, about the fate of a Polish Roma clan in occupied Europe during the Second World War.

Minds race and ideas flow. A Migrations theme could include the 1000 year journey by the Roma from India to Europe. Or Differing Lives could include the itinerant lifestyle. Costume would have immense mileage. And – hey – do I see the Roma flag included in that display of flags? There's a thought – what about 'Peoples without a Country' or ...

A Roma inclusive curriculum will pay huge dividends in many ways. If our pupils grasp the issues around 1000 years of exclusion, marginalisation and persecution, and what this does to the mindset of persecutor and persecuted, we will have educated them well.

A good practice school clears stumbling blocks

The need for effective induction procedures is accepted in Enfield secondary schools and there is much good practice. What is vital is that all staff – including, and perhaps especially, front line administrative staff – need to be aware of the double whammy faced by the Roma.

Knowledge and sensitivity are key. We should be knowledgeable about aspects and events that Roma prioritise and how these influence their lives. A key Roma value is that family and community come first. Clan events, not only weddings or funerals but also ordinary visits by relatives, are generally of paramount importance for Roma and often take priority over school attendance. Relatives and friends who visit for a few days may keep out of school. And when the house is full of guests there may well be scant time or space for the children to do their homework. Roma children may have family jobs, such as babysitting or interpreting, and these too can take precedence over school attendance. One family might send some of the children to school while regarding others as indispensable at home.

A self help culture characterises Roma families' behaviour. Parents tend to deal with their children's behavioural and health matters within the family. A 'troublemaker' may be kept away from school, and minor illness might be seen as a reason to keep a child at home. Such practice is often reinforced by the confusion regarding the procedure legitimising absence from school. In many Eastern European countries absence is first authorised with a sick note signed by a GP, after which it is no longer seen as the responsibility of the education authorities. So they may not realise that the rules of school attendance are different in the UK.

In sum, good practice in schools that is particularly helpful for Roma pupils is characterised by

- tolerating a flexible pattern of attendance building from part time to full time
- a school ethos of zero tolerance to bullying and racism that includes Roma
- flexibility in uniform requirements. School uniform differs greatly from the clothing Roma families traditionally wear. If the objective is to encourage attendance, it is pointless to send a child home because the trousers they are wearing are the wrong shade of blue

- accepting that jewellery is a fundamental part of Roma dress
- being willing to view attendance percentages in terms of pupil progress rather than externally imposed targets
- being willing and able to set aside time to fill in and explain forms – which should be clear and succinct
- generous use of translators
- a sensitive buddy system
- a flexible system that ensures sensitive allocation of new pupils to a form group – and readiness to change form if necessary.
- the opportunity for school staff to visit families at home.
- the use of local expertise in training and support. Traveller Education Services in many authorities have built up a wide knowledge base and experienced staff (Tyler, 2005, forthcoming) – it's always a good sign if we are invited in to provide inservice training.

And finally, even when schools operate the best practice, this needs to be underscored by cohesive, joined up inter-agency thinking at local and national level. Weeks of patient work can come to nothing when families are moved on. Often work is duplicated by different agencies, leaving families confused as to who is who, and what each is supposed to be doing. Or the issues aren't addressed because everybody thinks someone else is doing it. Keeping track of family movements to ensure children are accessing school demands a level of inter-agency support that rarely exists. One sometimes suspects that agencies are unwilling to pass information on but are instead watching over their shoulders lest they run up against data protection issues. (For models of inter-agency approaches see Green, 1999.)

In May 2004 eight Eastern European countries gained access to the European Union and the situation for Roma changed. Asylum seeking families who have been here since 2 October 2000 will generally be granted indefinite leave to remain. But there will still be challenges for the education system. Dedicated workers will be required for many years yet and they will need a keen understanding of current issues and strong determination to persevere. It is important that theses professionals do not allow the problems that arise at the interface of family and education system to hinder them in their work to ensure that these children have full access to the opportunities available to other pupils.

If a 'can do' attitude is needed anywhere, it is needed here. Indeed 'can do' should read 'must do' – we cannot afford to fail these children.

This poem is written by Claudia (15yrs), and appears in *Colours of Hope* (2003), by kind permission of the Roma Support Group (see Teaching Resources):

Fly

Those who are afraid
To fall never fly.
How will you ever know
If you never try?
Might just reach your
Goals
And your every dream.
You can never be sure.
If not,
You can learn
From the mistakes
You make.
At least you'll wonder
No more.

The saddest thing
Is a life never lived,
A desired task never
Tried,
Wishing stars
Never wished upon,
Left floating in the sky,
Dreams left as dreams,
Hopes and ambitions,
Pushed to the back of
One's mind.
If you never speak,
You'll never be heard.
If you don't seek,
You'll never find.

Never let them tell you
That you can't, couldn't
Or shouldn't.
Never give then the
Satisfaction
Of being the reason you
Wouldn't.
Never let their jealousy
Or disbelief
Be the reason you don't
Or won't
Try.
Don't let the only time
You ever really fly
Be the day you die

Claudia, age 15

I am indebted to my colleague Valentin Kovalenko for some of the historical information and notes on the situation that has led Roma to come to this country.

Background reading

General

Romany Refugees from Eastern Europe Camden Traveller Education Service 1999 (currently being revised)

Recent History

We are the Romany People University of Hertfordshire Press 2002
Bury Me Standing Chatto and Windus 1995
No Record of the Case European Roma Rights Center 1997
Sudden Rage at Dawn European Roma Rights Center 1996
Time of the Skinheads European Roma Rights Center 1997
A False Dawn University of Hertfordshire Press 1999
Between Past and Future University of Hertfordshire Press 2001

Porraimos (Holocaust)

Gypsies under the Swastika University of Hertfordshire Press 1995
Shared Sorrows University of Hertfordshire Press 2002
A Gypsy in Auschwitz London House 1999

Education

Denied a Future: The Right to Education of Gypsy and Traveller Children in Europe Save the Children 2001

The Roma Education Resource Book
www.osi.hu/iep/minorities/ResBook1/ResBookAll.htm 1999

Videos

Roma Asylum Seekers: A Learning Experience Education Bradford 2003
Equal Chances Save the Children Fund

Teaching resources (very few Roma specific materials available)
Colours of Hope The Roma Support Group 2004
PO Box 23610 London E7 0XB
020 8514 7820 07949 089 778
roma@supportgroup.freeserve.co.uk www.romasupportgroup.org.uk

KS2/3

Basic Words and Phrases for Teachers Working with Czech Children
Education Bradford 1999 (Teachers' Resource)

Porraimos: The Devouring Northants County Council 1999 (Book KS3/4)

Gypsies and the Holocaust ASET 2001(Teachers Pack KS3)

Gypsies and the Holocaust Kent County Council (Booklets/Posters (KS3/4)

5

WORKING WITH SOMALI BOYS IN A SECONDARY SCHOOL

'AN EDUCATING EXPERIENCE'

Mala German

Schools are not alone

Although the needs of some refugee[1] students can appear overwhelming, there is already much good practice in secondary schools and in some cases it has become part of the everyday ethos and curriculum (Ofsted, 2003; Rutter, 2003). Such practices include good admissions and induction procedures, effective communication with parents, buddy systems, using welcome and inclusion activities in class circle time and whole school PHSE programmes, exploring the nature of the refugee experience through the curriculum and citizenship programmes (Bolloten and Spafford, 2003; Lee, 2003). Refugee pupils generally demonstrate considerable resilience and such strategies effectively meet most of their needs. Good practice empowers them to achieve well in school and make good use of their first experience of a sensitive and contained learning environment. Support for schools for implementing such strategies usually falls under the remit of the borough's Ethnic Minority Achievement Advisory Team.

There are some refugee pupils, however, about whom teachers may become particularly concerned. The pupils may continue to appear isolated or withdrawn. Or they may present with acting out behaviours that could be communicating some experience of earlier or present difficulties. Such pupils are in need of a more targeted approach that addresses some of their psychosocial and emotional needs.

For their voices to be truly heard and their feelings and needs expressed, it is critical that they have access to a member of staff, community worker or parent who speaks their home language.

Schools should in the first instance be able discuss the needs of such pupils with their Educational Psychologist (EP). This EP may be able to offer support directly or to link up with the EP who has responsibility for developing such work in the Educational Psychology Service (EPS). Priority areas of work for educational psychologists include child protection, looked after children, pupils at risk of exclusion and asylum seeking/refugee students, as it is these groups who are recognised as the most socially vulnerable and excluded members of the community. EPSs have recently become more proactive in meeting the psychosocial needs of refugee students, and a number of services have either specialist teams or EPs with specialist responsibility. The latest government regulation (Ofsted, 2003) has recommended that it is the responsibility of the LEA to provide advice and guidance to schools on how to support refugee students who are experiencing psychological problems and trauma.

The local Child and Adolescent Mental Health Service (CAMHS) or Child Guidance Service may also have a specialist team or professionals with a brief to do outreach work in the community, who could also be approached for support[2]. Such outreach work is often considered preferable to clinic based work as it is within a context and surroundings that the youngsters are familiar with. This helps form a bridge between differing cultural interpretations of 'psychological support', as for many ethnic minority groups these concepts and such professionals will be alien to their own culture and may seem threatening at first.

This chapter describes the approach used by one north London mixed secondary comprehensive school. The school already had a number of good practice strategies in place, but became concerned particularly about the needs of the Somali students who were not only underachieving but were also having problems adjusting to the school culture and showed signs of emotional difficulties.

Somali achievement in schools

As a result of civil war in Somalia over the past 20 years Somalis have been arriving in the UK seeking asylum and there have been concerns regarding their underachievement in the British education system. Little research has been done on the achievement of Somali students in UK schools. Kahin (1997) reported on a preliminary survey conducted by Somalink in 1996, looking at 120 Somali pupils at sixteen schools. Somalink found that less than 30 per cent of the Somali pupils entered for GCSE in 1995/6 achieved grades A-C in 5 or more subjects compared with the national average of 43 per cent. In addition (Demie, 2001) research reminds us that students who are not fluent in English have restricted access to the National Curriculum and are therefore disadvantaged.

Background to the project

This project came about in response to a request from the headteacher and assistant principal for support from the borough's Child Guidance Service Refugee Team[3] regarding concerns about the needs of the school's Somali students. The CGS Refugee Team's EP and Somali Bilingual Family Liaison Officer initially met with the headteacher, and agreed that the first phase of the project would be a needs analysis of the Somali students, using focus group research methodology to identify current needs and concerns. The findings were fed back to the school's senior management team. This coincided with a new welcome centre in the school for newly arrived pupils, updating its induction and admissions policy and the class friends/buddy system with the support of the EMA advisory team. The school had just appointed a new EMA co-ordinator, who was keen to work with outside agencies to help develop the work of the department.

After discussing the findings, and in consultation with the headteacher and deputy, it was agreed in July 2002 that a support group was needed, focusing initially on the needs of the Somali boys in the school. Within a year the Somali girls were seen to be making use of new facilities the school had set up at the Welcome Centre, and a class friends system. But the staff remained concerned about the Somali boys, whom they saw as particularly vulnerable. So it was agreed that the CGS Refugee Team would work first with the Somali boys and then later with the girls.

In addition, the school staff reported that the project would meet the criteria for the DfES Pupil Mobility Project bid that the school successfully accessed. The school had also recently employed a male Somali teacher.

School profile

- of the 984 students on roll 37 per cent have English as an additional language and 16 per cent are new to English
- 27 per cent of the school population joined the school at a time other than the usual admission day
- the largest ethnic minority group in the school – 15 per cent of the school's population (150 pupils) – are Turkish/Kurdish
- approximately 300 children on the EMA register are from refugee families
- a high number of new admissions (60) had entered year 10

- 50 Somali pupils – 30 boys and 20 girls – make up the third largest ethnic minority in the school
- the school has an EMA team which has two teachers for the Somali and Turkish community, two learning support mentors, and an EMA co-ordinator

Using group work as an intervention to raise self esteem and achievement

Teachers work with groups all the time and are experienced at facilitating various types of groups. Group work may take the form of circle time, PHSE tutorial sessions or social skills groups. So work might be conducted with the whole year group, ranging through the form group, down to smaller groups for specific purposes and with a particular target student group. Many models are employed in group work, ranging from didactic structured social skills programmes to using therapeutic interventions which may involve specialists from outside agencies.

The group can be a powerful tool for promoting students' emotional development, learning, understanding and positive social interaction. Particularly for pupils who have just arrived at the school and have little English, anxious questions about school culture, local geographic culture, expectations, norms and misunderstandings can be resolved in a safe environment.

> A group is an environment in which people can observe what others do and say and then observe what happens next. Even when a person may appear to be doing nothing more than watching or listening, s/he might be noting events which have a particular meaning. For example someone who has always been afraid to make challenges may be observing others make challenges. A group is also an environment in which people can receive feedback from other members about their own behaviour or participation in the group. Receiving feedback from others in the group is one of its main advantages as a context for helping personal growth. (Greenhalgh, 1994, p.192)

However, groups can also present with challenges over the relationship between the pupils' individual identity and the identity of the group; the role of the facilitator is to try to resolve these tensions (Greenhalgh, 1994). It is not the remit of this chapter to discuss the psychological aspects of working with groups, but much has been written on the positive outcomes of using group work with adolescents in school (see e.g. Dwivedi, 1993). Where schools are co-facilitating groups with psychologists or group workers these aspects can be considered and worked with.

Planning and principles

It was decided that the project should be a pilot that would fall under the overall programme at the school to raise the achievement of its ethnic minority pupils. Through initial consultation, the school identified the difficulties they thought the Somali pupils were facing as relating to:

- having to deal with multiple losses from the asylum seeking/ refugee experience of family/friends, community support, economic support, home and culture
- experiencing difficulties, uncertainty and stress caused by the process of applying for asylum, and the legal difficulties involved
- the stresses of living in poor housing, temporary accommodation, having poor financial support and having to move several times over
- their lack of prior experience in any schooling system because of civil war in Somalia
- frustration and difficulties experienced in learning English in order to access the curriculum
- difficulties in making friendships in school
- their own poor behaviour in some cases

Principles

Although some staff thought initially that the group's function should be to address behavioural difficulties of the Somali boys, it was agreed that this might be perceived as too negative and that the boys would see the group as punishment[4]. Rather, the group was to be set up on positive principles to help them make sense of the school and its cultural context, expectations and needs. It was agreed that staff would aim for a supportive ethos, in which the boys could feel that there was some acknowledgement of the difficulties they might be facing. The project was ultimately called the Somali Boys' Support Group.

It was also agreed that the group should be cross phase and include positive role models by involving Somali youngsters who were doing well at the school. This was to encourage the sharing of experiences, and promote joint problem solving and learning from one another.

The project was set up to be run by the school and be part of normal curriculum delivery, such as PHSE, and pastoral support. In addition, there would be some incidental learning of English as the Somali teacher would be interpreting for the group.

- The group was to be facilitated by a member of school staff and the Educational Psychologist from the Child Guidance Service Refugee Team
- The Somali teacher and EMA Co-ordinator organised informing the parents and explaining the purpose of the group and project
- A supervision/feedback session should follow directly after each group session, so that the EMA team could pursue anything necessary and plan accordingly for the next session
- The facilitators and the EMA team would attend the supervision group
- Another EP (currently researching the needs of African Caribbean boys and raising achievement in secondary schools) also provided supervision
- The group would meet for six sessions for one hour (one lesson) at the end of the day
- The EMA co-ordinator would arrange matters with the school staff and facilitate pupil reminders

If this approach proved successful and met the pupils' needs, the staff would think about how else it might be applied, and the findings would help in planning for the Somali girls' support group.

Aims of the Somali Boys' Support Group project

- to provide a safe supportive environment where the boys' concerns could be discussed and listened to. Equal emphasis to be placed on strengths and difficulties that the boys themselves bring to discuss
- the role of the group facilitators would be to help the group explore the material the group members brought to them (both content and process)
- to develop the boys' listening and problem solving skills regarding the difficulties they faced
- to provide school staff with further insights – by means of supervision sessions – into the boys' weaknesses and strengths and the issues that might need taking up systemically or with a single individual.

Profiles of the students chosen

The EMA team co-ordinator chose the candidates for the group in consultation with school staff. All the boys had come from difficult asylum/refugee backgrounds and were separated from or had lost their fathers or other members of their family. Most lived with their mothers and siblings. Some were relatively new to English while others had lived in the UK for up to five years; two of the boys had fluent English language skills. Some spoke Swahili and Arabic in addition to Somali. As the group progressed all the boys except one reported that they had experienced temporary short-term exclusions for behavioural difficulties.

Pre-group planning and preparation

The original plan was for the group to meet during the spring term, so avoiding the busy exam period. But unfortunately the Somali teacher became ill and an interpreter[5] was sought. The Turkish EMA teacher offered to join the group as co-facilitator.

The EP for the CGS Refugee team offered some time with the interpreter to talk about the aims of the group and discuss roles. It was decided that the facilitation and responsibility for the group would be held by the EP and EMA teacher. This is in line with good practice for working with interpreters. It is also common for refugee support teams to offer training for interpreters or to employ members from the communities as bilingual family liaison workers to conduct joint work (Tribe and Raval, 2003). The interpreter was also booked for debriefing time so that any emotional issues or difficulties that might have arisen from what someone in the group had said could be discussed and appropriately dealt with.

Before the group sessions began, the boys were interviewed with the interpreter to explain the purpose and nature of the group and to see if they were interested in joining. All the boys interviewed expressed an interest in joining, although it was evident throughout the interviews that they were initially worried that they had been chosen for negative reasons. The boys were then asked whether they would like to join the group and if so, why. The following reasons were cited:

- I can help the little boys
- I could get more help with English
- I would like to be able to speak my language with other Somali boys
- It will help me and maybe I will be able to help others
- Because they are Somali and they get teased in school because they don't speak very good English, and I would like to help them
- If they extend my time I would like to join to learn from the other Somali boys
- You can talk about different stuff and share what your difficulties are
- To get to know people in the group

Meeting times

A series of six regular meetings was planned for the spring term but with the departure of the Somali teacher this was moved to the summer term. This proved not to be the best time of the year as the year 11 pupil could only attend two of the sessions as he had exams. Indeed the cross phase year group strategy proved problematic because of individual timetables, although the benefits were believed to outweigh the difficulties. Eventually we found a time that was convenient for all the boys.

Structure of the group

In the first session the boys were invited to create their own rules for the group. There was much discussion over the need for rules in the group, in school and in life, and also some discussion about the cultural differences between the UK and Somalia. The boys came up with the following Group Rules:

1. No swearing
2. One person to speak at a time
3. When one person speaks the rest of the group listens
4. Respect each other's opinion
5. Respect for people whatever country they come from or language they speak
6. No fighting or bullying
7. Everything in the room is confidential (unless you may be in danger of harm)
8. We should try to be on time and not be late (this was added after session 2)

The boys also shared their perceptions of the purpose of the group. Each session began with warm up activities designed to improve social interaction and listening skills. Next, the boys went through the group rules. They were then encouraged to use the space to bring any issues they themselves wished to discuss with the group. This space was used surprisingly well and at first a main area for discussion was their inadequate English, being new at school and how to make friends. Over the six sessions the boys raised discussion about the following:

- feeling stupid when you can't speak English
- feeling alone and having no friends
- how to make friends
- bullying and being bullied
- 'cussing'
- fighting, peer pressure

- exploring the meaning of the group and school rules
- the differences between the expectations of behaviour towards adults in Somalia and in the UK
- difficulties accessing lessons when you don't understand

The boys were encouraged to use problem-solving skills and to share their experiences of how they had tackled difficulties. The empathic thinking and sharing that took place was impressive. Sometimes things were difficult, as the boys were obviously competing for space to talk and their patience was tried further by having to give the interpreter a chance to finish. The mix of ages and experience – including experience of living in the UK – seemed to work effectively. In one session the interpreter was late so one of the boys offered to translate, and this did cause some difficulty as some of the boys were impatient with those who had fewer English language skills.

Each group session would end with a few minutes in which the boys reviewed what they had found useful in the session or identified a word to express their feelings about it. The boys were entitled to pass on this but, again surprisingly, they engaged well with the activity. The consistency of the format provided containment and allowed for any unresolved issues in the group to be shared.

Supervision and reflection time

One key successful component of the project was that the group facilitators, interpreter and EMA co-ordinator spent time after every session reflecting on the content and process of the group. Supervision of these discussions was facilitated by another educational psychologist. This meant that the issues the boys raised which needed to be taken up within the school were revealed, as well as the emotional content they brought. The group facilitators were also encouraged to reflect on their own feelings during the group session, with a view to providing insights and helping to make sense of the boys' feelings and the issues they had raised. Educational psychologists are trained to help teachers reflect and provide support on understanding the emotional context of their interactions with their pupils. In particular the painful feelings evoked when working with refugee pupils require support and reflection time for the staff involved.

Communicating the aims of the project with the rest of the school

A critical aspect to the successful running and organisation of the project was the need for the EMA co-ordinator to feed back to the senior management team the progress of the project and to communicate clearly to all the staff what the aims and purpose of the group were and which pupils were taking part. The EMA co-ordinator provided reminders and additional support, to make sure the boys knew when and where to attend.

How the boys perceived the support group

The boys were interviewed at the end of the project with the help of the Somali interpreter. This summary of some of their responses shows the key themes that emerged.

Bullying and fighting

> The information I learned, the things we learned about bullying
>
> I learned something about bullying.
>
> We learned important things like [about] bullying and fighting.
>
> The things we learned throughout the period, like(about) bullying. If someone tries to do something unfair to you which they shouldn't, how you can handle that and how you can ignore it
>
> If someone tries to take money off you how you can report that to the teachers.
>
> I think the rules we learned and all the things we talked about in the group.

Understanding the school system

> How to report and complain to the teachers, these are things that I didn't know or didn't understand because of my English.
>
> It was an educating experience ... I was ignorant before.
>
> The others were aware of how to behave in a school setting. I was not aware before.

Social skills

> To treat people with respect and how to cope with people.
>
> Talking to people and being nice to people the way you should.
>
> We got to know each other in the group.

Somali boys

> It was useful to see how other Somali boys were coping.
>
> Good to have a group for Somali boys because some don't know English or how the school or the system works. You could practice and learn how to make friends in school and in the class.
>
> It's hard for Somali boys who don't speak English.
>
> If there were other countries in the group ... mmm ... there may have been fighting in the group.
>
> The group helped me with my own ideas.

When asked to reflect on what they thought could have improved the group, the boys said:

> If people were to talk more about their personal experiences we can put them together and make one collective thought in terms of problems we experience in school.
>
> It was fine as it was ... When are we getting our certificates?
>
> The Somali boys' group is a good idea. It is a good place for us to learn about things we don't know and improve our English.
>
> More time. I think there should be another group.
>
> There were other Somali boys who could have been in the group.
>
> I liked being in the group. But I did not like to miss my lesson.

All the boys wanted to be part of a subsequent group, except one who felt concerned that the experience should be available to other Somali students in the school.

Staff evaluation

The EMA staff reported that they had noticed improvements in the motivation and self esteem of a number of the boys who participated. Ahmed had been at risk of permanent exclusion but is now successfully included into the school and is accessing the curriculum. The EMA Turkish teacher who co-facilitated observed that through the group he was able to observe a side to the students he had not seen before and to learn about the issues that were most pertinent for the boys themselves.

No questionnaires or surveys were conducted with other members of staff as the main aim was to see if the Somali boys themselves perceived this project as useful. An evaluation that included teacher and parent perceptions before and after the programme would be valuable for further work. So would a self esteem questionnaire for the participants. The EMA staff reported that the use of the supervision sessions gave them time to reflect on not just the needs of the target group but also on the universal issues that affected other pupils from ethnic minority and refugee backgrounds.

The staff also reported that the students responded well to a special assembly at which they were presented with certificates for participating in the group. In the second phase of the project, the senior management team will discuss the findings of the pilot programme to see how to embed the work into the PHSE or induction programme for newly arrived pupils as part of normal school curriculum delivery.

Conclusion

It was evident that the project was perceived by the boys as helping to meet their emotional and social needs. Its success was due largely to the commitment and excellent organisational skills of the Ethnic Minority Achievement team and particularly the co-ordinator. The project was set up as a positive school activity for the boys to be part of, and the way that opportunities were provided for boys to give their views and ask questions about the group before they became formally involved also contributed to its success. Providing access to a person who can speak their home language enabled the boys to express their thoughts and feelings in a coherent way. Our findings highlight the importance of access to support of this kind in schools.

A number of areas of difficulty and concern were identified and discussed in the group. Clearly, the boys thought they had a safe forum in which to discuss them, thanks to the group. Mixing the year groups and including successful Somali pupils along with those at some risk was also helpful, as inexperienced pupils got to hear how the more experienced boys handled issues. The older boys were also able to reflect on their own experience of starting school and thus helped the younger members not to make the same mistakes.

Even though the pupils came from different socio-economic origins, status and positions in the conflict in Somalia, they demonstrated that they could deal with differences in attitudes and perspectives. As the group sessions progressed, a healthy tolerance of difference grew. The boys had also to deal with the loss of their Somali teacher who had been involved in setting up the group. Given that all the pupils had experienced loss or separation from their fathers, this was acutely painful for them, but again the group provided a forum in which to deal safely with these feelings.

This account has sought to give teachers an insight into how work of this nature can be carried out in schools with the support of the educational psychologist or other support services provided by the authority. It is important for teachers to understand that such work does not necessarily fall within the parameters of special educational needs, but is located within the remit of raising achievement of pupils who are vulnerable because of their asylum/refugee experience. Refugee children and young people who are dealing with multiple losses, changes, separations, poor housing and poverty may be exhibiting signs of difficulty which are normal reactions to abnormal experiences. The school can be a powerful and containing environment for refugee pupils. Within the safe environment it creates, group work can do much to foster emotional growth and learning and consequently raise the achievement of not only refugee pupils but all vulnerable pupils.

Notes

1 I use the term refugee synonymously with asylum seeker (those applying for refugee status), those who have been granted Humanitarian Protection or Discretionary Leave to Remain, and those who have Indefinite Leave to Remain (ILR i.e. full refugee status)

2 Some Child Guidance Service or CAMHS have the EPS as an integral part or have EPs employed in their multi-disciplinary team

3 In Enfield the Child Guidance Service has a specialist multi-disciplinary team funded by health and education that promotes outreach work by supporting the needs of asylum seekers and refugees in the community. It offers INSET and training for workers supporting refugees, offers individual therapeutic support, group work and projects in schools and community organisations and ethnic minority organisations, and conducts action research.

4 Interestingly the Somali boys themselves chose to discuss behaviour and this was a regular recurring theme during the project.

5 Our CGS Bilingual Family Liaison Officer had left the team to train as a Social Worker and we had a vacancy at the time of this project. It was thought that rather than delay the project it would be better to go ahead with an interpreter and offer some pre-briefing time to establish roles, boundaries and responsibilities.

6

'OH, MRS YIANNI YOU ARE A GOOD BOY'

TRAINING TEACHING ASSISTANTS TO SUPPORT ETHNIC MINORITY PUPILS

Janet Campbell

I may not have got a job in an office earning thousands, but I have got a job working with EAL children, whom I love supporting and I'm using my Turkish language to help the children during their time in school. I have built a very good relationship with both the children and their parents. Encouraging them to use their Turkish language at all times and assuring parents that their children will develop the English language as time goes by ... For the first time in my life, I feel valued for what I am, and feel very proud of being Turkish.

Su had just finished a one year Specialist Teaching Assistant course for Ethnic Minority Achievement (STA EMA), during which issues of language and identity, teaching and learning and the support role of teaching assistants in the classroom were explored. Like many of the bilingual TAs on the course, Su had faced difficulties as a child at school because of her language and ethnicity.

The course had been set up to respond to the changing situation in schools. With the devolvement of the grant for ethnic minority achievement, schools were employing more teaching assistants. When the STA EMA course was publicised, it drew an enthusiastic response from schools who wanted their teaching assistants trained, whether or not they were employed under the EMA grant. Many of the schools who have only recently admitted bilingual pupils have never had a specialist teacher but class teachers rely on the support of TAs to offer small group or individual attention to pupils learning English. Many TAs in this situation started the course believing that pupils new to English should not be in ordinary lessons, especially in Years 5 or 6. 'How can you include a newly arrived Arabic speaker in a lesson on *Macbeth*?' they ask. By the end of the course, those same TAs were proudly demonstrating the strategies they and their class teachers used to promote the inclusion of bilingual pupils, even when studying *Macbeth*.

The teaching assistants were asked to build up a portfolio of tasks, including doing a case study of one or two focus pupils (with the parents' permission). The case study noted the pupil's home language and use of English; a reading assessment; a detailed series of classroom observations to identify their learning priorities and establish support strategies; and finally, an assessment of the pupils' progress in English and the curriculum at the end of the year.

In addition to the case study, the TAs were asked to try out practical activities suggested on the course. They made 'Welcome' albums. They made whole school displays celebrating diversity. They made puppets and games to support literacy. They made practical resources to support numeracy. Most of all, they responded to the idea of making and using story boxes[1] to stimulate storytelling and writing. When the portfolios of work were submitted for assessment, we were astonished by the quality, and quantity, of the work.

Frances, a Specialist Teaching Assistant who is now a leading TA and mentor at her school, wrote about story boxes:

> I think one of the ways talk works best is through using props such as story boxes. It develops and expands children's vocabulary and can lead them to reading more ... If you volunteer to scribe for them it takes the pressure off and relaxes them. They then start to involve you by asking your opinion and then you can start asking questions and stretching their thoughts and imagination even wider ... You can see that even after a few sessions they are beginning to see themselves as story writers/tellers, more so the ones who were adamant that they couldn't do it – some of the best stories can come from them. A new trick I am using at the moment is to spray the inside with perfume – it opens up a whole new route of conversation.

Students are offered a variety of set reading between taught sessions as part of the private study requirement of the course. Selected texts range from *Being Bilingual* by Safder Alladina (1995), which is aimed at parents and carers as well as teachers, to a chapter from Shirley Clarke's *Unlocking Formative Assessment (2001)*

which challenges some of the accepted practices which pay 'lip service to self-esteem, contributing to a culture in which self-esteem increases most for those children who already have high self-esteem and where self-esteem 'rewards' are inevitably applied unevenly.'

Clarke's chapter generated a good deal of discussion at the following meeting, as teaching assistants started to talk about the complexities of classroom practice. Another session which stimulates high interest is about 'Community'. Here issues of race equality and refugees are raised. Jill Rutter's book, *Supporting Refugee Children in 21st Century Britain* (2003) provides an excellent introduction to the background experiences of pupils arriving newly in school and to the ways in which schools can work with parents and communities for the benefit of the pupils. Chapter 11, 'Home and Community Links' is particularly relevant to TAs, as they are often in a good position to develop home-school links. It helps if they are bilingual, even if their own language is not that of the families they support. At an evaluation meeting one headteacher suggested that perhaps the set reading was 'too difficult' for teaching assistants. His remark was vociferously repudiated by the TAs, many of whom asserted that the reading was an enjoyable part of the course.

As the teaching assistants were observing their pupils' progress, we were observing changes in them. Over the year there was a definite sense of growth in their self-confidence about their ability to express opinions in the group and also to make decisions in the classroom that would benefit the pupils.

Andie was working with a group of Year 2 pupils who were writing poems about themselves, based on James Berry's poem, 'One' (*Only one of ME,* selected poems, 2004).

> I read through *Only One of Me* and the children spoke about themselves. Anna, who is from Kosovo, noticed a beautiful red sequinned dress in the dressing up clothes hamper nearby. She kept looking at it. She said she liked dancing and that she could dance if she wore that dress. I said she could wear it and also the tap shoes. Anna danced around, turning and tapping. I showed her a mirror and she danced some more. Then she sat down to draw a picture of herself in the red dress, and wrote:

No one can dance like me
In my shiny red dress
Nobody plays like me
In my beautiful tick tack shoes
How I twist around in my dress

The quality of the work owes much to the partnership and trust between the class teacher and her experienced assistant. In primary schools, where teaching assistants have been employed for a long time, partnerships of this kind have had time to mature, especially in the Early Years. Good relationships with parents and the community have also been developed. Nese, a Turkish speaking teaching assistant, was recently singled out for praise by Ofsted inspectors for her work with pupils and parents. In her school Nese acts as an interpreter for parents and uses Turkish to support newly arrived pupils when they are settling in. She also has storytelling sessions in Turkish which are enjoyed by all the pupils, whatever languages they speak. Every year Nese organises a Children's Day celebration which celebrates the diversity of the school population and encourages all the parents to participate.

Teaching assistants have been encouraged to develop their personal skills for the benefit of the pupils. While working in Year 6 with a Somali refugee, Karen was aware that the withdrawal group which had been set up as support for Mohamed was inappropriate but felt powerless to change the situation. A change in policy gave Karen the opportunity to express her concern – and Mohamed and another refugee pupil were able to stay in the class, where they made progress in English and other areas of the curriculum.

As Karen observed, 'Mohamed has come on in leaps and bounds because he has lessons that are structured and scaffolded to help him learn.'

As a teaching assistant, Karen had the opportunity to build up a more personal relationship with Mohamed than the class teacher and that relationship contributed to Mohamed's gradual integration into the school. His account of his experience in Somalia, written as part of an exercise to practise for SATs, demonstrates how far he had come in trusting the adults supporting him. This is Mohamed's story:

> one day they going holiday in AFRICA and they enjoy and they decide if they can stay, but they child don't want to stay in AFRICA. Her mum said why are you don't want to stay here. Because we only stay in this country 3 month and we do not no what happen. Maybe this few we they choose a president and we don't now what is going to be happening may they as going to fight. They is no going to say this don't kill this family because they just visiter. They don't have choice they just kill. After they child talking them the next day they start to but they close in they bag as quickly as possible.

> Suddenly they heard the bom, they start to cry. Her mum said what happen is there coming to kill us. And the house which they stay, is starting to broking they running over the house. And they don't now where they going.

More than fifty teaching assistants have completed the course and it is over-subscribed for its third year, especially as the course content has been expanded to include TAs in secondary schools. The work submitted in portfolios has demonstrated the TAs' extremely high level of commitment to both pupil progress and their own learning. A few of the TAs have gone on to higher education via various routes: two on work based study programmes leading to degree and qualified teacher status, one on a Foundation degree course and another on a BSc course. All have told us that the specialist course gave them encouragement to go back to education for themselves. For others, the course is satisfying enough in itself, giving them a sense of professionalism and enhanced status in their schools.

Increasingly, teaching assistants are being employed in secondary schools, either directly through the EMA grant or as part of the workforce remodelling programme. These TAs are often asked to support newly arrived students in school and greatly appreciate the training offered in respect of English language acquisition and early literacy learning. The course content has been adjusted to include aspects of the secondary context but the TAs are actually benefiting from learning about primary practice. The session on reading, for instance, is subtitled *Where's Spot?* to *Spotlight Science* to encompass the entire process: from pre-reading skills to skimming and scanning for information in non fiction texts. By the end of the course the TAs will be able to:

- run induction programmes for newly arrived students, releasing EMA teachers for classroom partnership teaching
- contribute to assessment for learning by giving feedback to teachers based on their knowledge of the students
- contribute to the development of literacy for early learners of English by using strategies which complement the National Strategy (book sharing, story boxes, visual literacy)
- liaise with ethnic minority parents.

The cross phase course is being developed further as a pilot for the DfES Aiming High initiative.

The main beneficiaries of the course are the pupils who are supported by these talented TAs. Working with ethnic minority pupils is satisfying, if not that rewarding financially. Christine sums up for many in her final report on the progress of one of her pupils:

It has been an absolute joy to witness the development of Deniz's language and understanding and the way he enjoys every new experience. When it snowed earlier this year Deniz couldn't believe it and later tore up pieces of white paper and threw them in the air saying, 'Mrs Yianni snow falling'. I'd like to leave you with praise I received from Deniz: 'Oh, Mrs Yianni you are a good boy!'

I now have to do some work explaining gender.

Note

1 The use of story boxes is based on Helen Bromley's work. Teaching assistants were asked to read three articles: 'Storytelling. Having a go with the box (1) (2) (3)' from *Primary English Magazine*. January/February 1999

7

LISTENING TO PUPILS

STRIVING TO SUCCEED – AN ACTION RESEARCH PROJECT ON HIGHLY ACHIEVING AFRICAN CARIBBEAN PUPILS

Alison Heap

> In many LEAs there is an uncertainty which verges on helplessness about what are the effective strategies to improve attainment for some groups. There is for instance a worrying ignorance generally, about how to raise the attainment of Black Caribbean boys. *Raising the Attainment of Minority Ethnic Pupils* Ofsted 1999

As Ethnic Minority Achievement advisers within the Enfield School Improvement Service, we undertook local action research in 2002. Firstly, we read up on the current research literature about the urgent need to address the underachievement of African Caribbean young people overall in UK schools. We also talked to Black teachers, parents and other professionals. Secondly, we interviewed Black pupils in Years 12 and 13, asking them to reflect on their successful experience of schooling and to identify ways in which schools could support African Caribbean pupils and maximise their achievement. The resulting report, *Striving to Succeed* (2002), was then published in Enfield for secondary schools and the LEA.

This chapter focuses on the recommendations the pupils made and tries to show how schools, the LEA and the voluntary sector have responded or intend to respond to each of the recommendations. Each section begins with key quotations from the pupils we interviewed and the recommendations they made.

Understanding and affirming every pupil

'I can do something with my life rather than just run or play football'

'...being able to do all the things you want to do .. being given a chance'

The pupils wanted schools and teachers to

be aware of children's successes in their earlier schooling

recognise and build on the strengths and talents of the whole child

raise awareness of ethnic diversity in schools and in wider society

provide opportunities to talk about identity and ethnicity in the curriculum

ensure that pupils are prepared for and can seek individual support at times of change

develop peer mentoring of younger pupils by older pupils

recognise that Black pupils are keen to support each other and encourage positive peer support networks

maintain pupils' positive commitment to and pride in their school

encourage pupils to reflect on the advantages and disadvantages of attending single sex or church schools

develop pupils' awareness of their own learning styles and those of others

foster a culture of respect within the school community

Like everyone consulted in the research, the pupils had a great deal to say about self-esteem and identity. They wanted to challenge what they saw as the overwhelmingly negative images of the Black community in 'media sources, mythology, gossip and hearsay', and they understood that this constant diet influences everyone 'with and without their knowledge'.

They wanted teachers to be willing to trust young people more to 'do the right thing'. They wanted more opportunities to be heard, and to contribute to and influence school life. They wanted more role models for Black young people in schools and better understanding of the social pressures they face. They were particularly critical of what they saw as short term fads to deal with disaffected pupils and wanted to see more long term innovation and support. They asked for greater curriculum choice, more extra curricular opportunities and for school generally to be more fun.

The pupils thought there were many ways that schools could affirm to Black pupils' self-esteem and sense of identity. They felt that schools should be more aware of children's successes in their primary schooling and also in the wider community. Several schools in the LEA conduct extensive surveys and interviews with pupils on their admission to the school. Teaching staff thus receive as rounded a picture as possible of the new pupils, including their community activities, interests, musical or other extra curricular involvement. Staff can thus pick up on pupils as individuals and this seems to have a very positive effect on the pupils themselves.

The Pupil Level Annual School Census introduced nationally in 2002 means that all schools now have a detailed profile of their pupils' ethnicity and language backgrounds. This information can be used to promote more dialogue between schools, parents and communities. It can also help to ensure that schools are getting their full entitlement to grants such as the Ethnic Minority Achievement grant. The data can be used on a daily basis to inform the teaching of PSHE, to provide useful material for assemblies and to support and monitor parental and community involvement.

Initiatives that have proved their worth

- Excellence in Cities and Education Action Zones are being used to support much innovative work in local schools. Schools are using this additional funding to support them with work on issues as diverse as boys' achievement, out of school activities and learning styles – all of which can positively affect the educational experiences of Black pupils. Learning Mentors are making a significant difference in many schools. They provide individual and group support to pupils who are struggling or causing concern and often serve as role models from under-represented communities in the schools. They also give valuable feedback to schools about pupils' views on the school culture and ethos – although sometimes schools may find their comments difficult to take.

- Supplementary schools' links with mainstream schools are being strengthened so that understanding and co-operation is developing and barriers between these two long separated strands of education are at last being broken down. Now each is becoming more appreciative of the other's valuable and complex role.

- Voluntary organisations such as the Windsor Fellowship offer services to support schools and pupils in education. They allow pupils to make collective comments about their schooling and this prevents the unsatisfactory scenario in which pupils who are already in trouble try to question the system. As well as supporting individual pupils and helping them to stay on track, such organisations can give useful staff training and valuable feedback to the school about the kinds of problems pupils are encountering and how these might be addressed.

- Pupils wanted teachers to act quickly to support pupils if their behaviour and/or performance started to deteriorate. One response has been to develop strategies to support transition between the primary and the secondary phase in the Enfield Education Action Zone. That teachers in secondary schools should have high expectations of their African Caribbean intake was seen as crucial. Several London Challenge pilot initiatives in the LEA's schools are looking at this issue in depth.

- The consistent use of circle time in many primary schools allows children the chance to share their achievements and strengths and to build on them. Circle time is less developed in Enfield secondary schools, although pilots have shown that it can give a valuable opportunity for older children, too, to talk in a safe and depersonalised way about all sorts of difficulties they encounter. Bullying, racist incidents and name calling can all be sensitively discussed so that children develop a common language and positive collective strategies. In this way they come to understand what is acceptable and what is not – and why.

- Pupils want more opportunities to learn and talk about ethnicity and diversity in classrooms and the Citizenship Framework provides the opportunity to do this. The authority's EMA Team recently developed and provided to all secondary schools a unit of work for Year 7 PSHE about cultural diversity in Britain, encouraging pupils to reflect on their own identity. Pupils were asked to place speech bubbles about migration in chronological order. Some schools also have activity days which are specifically focused on community projects or research, providing a wide variety of community organisations with opportunities to showcase their work.

- Work on Black History Month has been developing fast in Enfield schools lately. The Enfield Black History Month Resources Fair and INSET sessions have inspired many teachers. Work done by pupils has been displayed in local libraries and public places, to great acclaim. Publicity in the local papers and the involvement of councillors has also helped to dispel long-standing, if unwitting, negative images.

- Conferences on Black Achievement have been organised for all interested members of the community, with awards being given to pupils. These events have created new opportunities to hear and discuss current research and ideas.

- Many of the young people interviewed for the *Striving to Succeed* report were keen that pupils should be encouraged to show commitment to and take pride in their schools. The longest established and highest performing schools have always been good at this, but recently other schools have made progress in this area too. Strategies have included explicitly developing year teams or house systems to encourage pupils to have a strong identification with their school.

That teacher said 'I've seen a spark and I'm not going to let it go out' and I'll gladly go along with her because she really cares (Ofsted, 1999).

Dealing with racism

'People who suffer because of who they are, will dislike themselves and that's the worst thing I can imagine'

'it's the way they (teachers) talk to you and the way they look down on you'

'I think that exclusion has something to do with racism. Some people can deal with it and some can't and it breaks them down and pushes them to do things'

The pupils wanted schools and teachers to:

ensure that everyone in the school community is confident about and committed to procedures for dealing with racism and racist incidents

recognise the pressures of racism and street culture which pupils may experience and offer support or perhaps second chances

investigate thoroughly all the circumstances leading up to each incident

Pupils from one school felt that racism was dealt with effectively but those from the three other schools talked about staff being ineffective in such circumstances. They said that pupils often had to follow up incidents themselves. Most Black pupils felt they were treated differently from other ethnic groups and told us that teachers needed more training and that teachers don't understand what racism means to them. Several felt that schools needed to deal more effectively with inter-racial incidents in particular i.e. those between members of different ethnic minorities. Pupils identified the main causes of exclusion as: 'lack of self-esteem', 'pupils' needs to be acknowledged' and 'being stereotyped'.

Some pupils talked about how racism made Black pupils feel their 'power' had been taken away from them and that consequently pupils felt the need to group together to deal with this and to look after each other.

When discussing peer pressure, pupils talked about Black young people wanting to feel superior so as to counteract their frequent experience of racism and being talked down to. They said also that teachers perceived groups of Black pupils as being up to no good and therefore needing to be split up. They said that it was easy to become stereotyped because of who you mixed with. They talked about gangs and clearly regarded gangs as families that look out for each other. 'You feel equal when you are in a gang', they told us.

Pupils wanted schools to ensure that everyone in the school community is confident about and committed to procedures for dealing with racism and racist incidents. The Enfield EMA team had already worked with colleagues from the LEA School Improvement Service to provide schools with a recommended set of guidelines for dealing with racist incidents, known as 'Stand Up To Racism'. The guidelines suggest that senior staff should monitor incidents, identify patterns and initiate proactive whole school responses wherever possible. Figure 1 opposite shows an extract from these guidelines. It is a grid on which school senior managers can identify patterns or trends in racist incidents. They can then plan whole school responses, short and longer term, to the patterns identified. Schools have used this guidance to help them review their existing procedures and the EMA team has worked in staff meetings, particularly with primary schools, discussing the issues involved and trying to improve the confidence of staff to handle racist incidents. Recently, training has been provided for non-teaching staff to explore the ways schools can address cultural bias and race equality in the curriculum.

A good many schools in Enfield had a Race Equality policy well before the Race Relations Amendment Act came into force in 2002, and they review their identified priorities annually as part of their school plan. The Enfield Racial Incidents Action Group is also keen to work more closely with Enfield schools to prevent and counteract racial incidents in schools and in the wider community.

Many of the interviewees considered it extremely important that all the circumstances leading up to the incident be investigated thoroughly. Several pupils had had personal experience of incidents they felt had not been handled fairly. In some instances the background had been inadequately investigated; in others it had been wrongly assumed that certain background information was irrelevant. All knew of cases which had been badly handled and where salient details and previous history had been ignored or given insufficient weight. Such inadequate responses often caused resentment and led to situations that undermined the faith of Black pupils in the disciplinary processes. Where these difficulties are being overcome and trust rebuilt, it is senior managers and learning mentors who are leading the way. Activities like circle time can also allow pupils to find ways to talk about such grievances and discuss ways forward in an impersonal and objective way.

Enfield Recommendations for Managing Racial Incidents — January 2000

Prompts for Analysis of Racial Incidents Monitoring Log

	Observations	Short term action	Long term action
Time and location Where incidents occur, what times of day, circumstances (eg after PE), etc	• School field (3 incidents in 1 week)	• extra senior staff on duty after school	• Y12/13 buddy system
Recipients/perpetrators Gender, year group/s, ethnicity, new arrivals etc	• 2 incidents involving 8E (P) • 3 incidents involving Somali students (V)	• review earlier log - 8E ? • meeting of Somali students (interpreter needed)	• meeting of 8E teachers (discuss class culture, assembly, PSHE, Circle Time)
Nature of reporting Timing, adequate details, who reports, who doesn't	• 4 out of 5 incidents outside lessons • 3 out of 5 reported next day or later • 2 out of 5 – same SMSA	• review earlier log – trends confirmed	• SMSAs meeting (time needed for reporting ?) • Staff meeting reporting incidents
Nature of follow-up Appropriate action, punishments, consistency	• overuse of detentions?	• See Ms. Baker re same punishment for V & P?	• making behaviour policy and practice consistent – Staff meeting ?

Figure 1

Above all, pupils wanted to see a culture of respect within the school community. The fact that they mention this suggests they feel it is lacking. Schools which are overcoming these feelings are doing so by being overtly antiracist and dealing effectively with all racist incidents. In such schools, all the pupils feel they have a voice. They run the assemblies and bring the issues that concern them to the fore. Community links are positively encouraged and innovation in working with parents and community is constantly on the agenda. Classroom codes are collectively agreed and enforced.

Curriculum

'the more interactive the lessons are the better'

'Schools need to find out what children are interested in'

The pupils wanted schools and teachers to

provide more careers support and advice – and from early on

provide more opportunities for developing problem-solving and decision-making skills in the curriculum

ensure that teachers are vigilant and take supportive action if pupils start to 'slide'

provide a wider range of curricular and social opportunities

review curriculum opportunities in Year 12 and 13 in the light of students' interests and preferences

Successful curriculum initiatives

- Much of what has been reported here is relevant also to the curriculum. In many primary and some secondary schools in Enfield, projects focusing explicitly on raising career aspirations for specific ethnic groups have proved popular and successful. These have reflected on the nature of success, engaging pupils in confidence building activities, drama and role play, and offering a wider range of role models. And the parents are always involved.
- National Strategy initiatives on challenge, engagement and thinking skills are increasing awareness amongst teachers of diversity of learning styles and the value of visual or auditory and kinaesthetic approaches in the classroom. The consequent professional development is positively affecting the classroom experiences of many pupils. Several secondary schools now regularly arrange theatre group productions focusing on issues around racial identity. These are linked to their PSHE programmes to allow pupils to spend time during school exploring the issues raised in the drama.

- The early findings of projects such as those funded by the London Challenge suggest that improved monitoring and data collection and the consequent awareness of underachieving pupils or groups, along with the increased confidence in addressing these pupils' needs, are paying off. The pupils' behaviour and motivation has improved and, consequently, their performance.
- Many schools in Enfield have considerably expanded their out-of-hours programmes for pupils in recent years, not only by allocating more time but also by extending the range of activities on offer. Informal monitoring by teachers suggests that pupils who customarily took no part in out of school activities are increasingly becoming involved in them.

* Certain schools have recently had great success as a result of rethinking their curriculum and offering new courses at Key Stage 5 or extending courses with good take-up by particular groups of ethnic minority pupils. Staff in these schools have reflected on the possibility that they stereotype certain ethnic groups and have responded to pupil feedback, monitored course take-up more closely and experimented with new courses, to try to break down any stereotypical thinking.

Parents and community

> 'My mum is always pushing me. She makes sacrifices for me and I can't let that go to waste'
>
> 'There needs to be more dialogue between pupils and teachers about all sorts of things that go on in schools'

The pupils wanted schools and teachers to

explore new ways of working in partnership with parents and carers

be aware of and make links with the outside activities of parents, carers and pupils at places such as supplementary schools, clubs, churches

involve parents and carers in discipline matters as early as possible.

The next chapter focuses on links with parents and the community.

> Memories are long and you have to be pro-active. (Ofsted 1999)

Conclusions

The publication of our local research on Black achievement, *Striving to Succeed*, alongside the guidance and initiatives from central government over the past few years, has provided additional impetus to the work in Enfield schools. Pupils themselves have responded positively to the publication. Many teachers and schools are gaining confidence and enthusiasm about addressing the needs of these pupils.

The response from Black parents and the Black community has been encouraging. The Enfield Caribbean Association held a meeting to discuss the report and its recommendations with the Director of Education and council members and this led to a joint working group being set up. Within the LEA, a working group called EAST (Enfield African Caribbean Support Team) has been successfully revived. It brings together a range of professionals from schools, libraries and the School Improvement Service. EAST has organised a successful conference on African Caribbean Achievement and was central to the success of the Black History Month initiatives. An Enfield Ethnic Minority Education Practitioners' Group offers support and a voice to Black and ethnic minority teachers.

Great strides have been taken in an area of London where concerns about Black pupils have not been consistently addressed in the past and there is certainly potential for further progress. The more open the dialogue between pupils, parents and all staff about the issues outlined in this chapter, the more successful we will all be in ensuring that all pupils achieve the best possible success.

> Black pupils felt ... that the Head was willing to listen to ... their point of view. More importantly, she was willing to do something about their sense of alienation and rejection. This was critical to the process of change ... in the school. (Ofsted, 1999)

Notes

Excellence in Cities is a national programme funded by the DfES to support many urban school through initiatives such as City Learning (ICT) Centres, Learning Mentors and Aiming Higher, to encourage under-represented groups into higher education

Education Action Zones are created to attract additional funding to raise achievement in clusters of schools facing socio-economic disadvantage.

Circle time can be used to develop self-esteem and positive behaviour in all pupils. Sessions are held regularly, to address common issues and build a successful school community.

8

LISTENING TO PARENTS

STRIVING TO SUCCEED – AN ACTION RESEARCH PROJECT ON HIGHLY ACHIEVING AFRICAN CARIBBEAN PUPILS

Marcia Sinclair

It takes a whole village to educate a child

When I was in West Africa, I travelled from the south of Ghana to a village in the northern region called Mole. I was exploring the village when an elderly man greeted me, welcomed me and asked 'Who are you?' I gave my name and said that I was over on holiday from England. 'Yes, but who *are* you', he demanded. He was joined by some children and an elderly lady. I offered my name yet again and told him what I did for a living. 'Yes', they said, 'but who are you?'

I finally understood what he wanted. He wanted to know my ancestry – my family, tribe and language – the things that would place me in context of all those who had come before me. At that moment I realised how ill prepared I was to answer the old man's question.

The encounter reminded me of my own upbringing in the Caribbean. If I answered the same question there, my surname would automatically link me with a region on the island and my family status. There are similarities between the two countries. As in Africa, the people of the Caribbean have a strong sense of community and many organised social events are deeply steeped in their traditions. Extensive rituals for births, deaths, marriages, the building of houses and other major events are conducted with great care and proper attention to tradition. The rites of the past co-exist with the ways of doing things in the modern era.

Returning from West Africa to England and to work, I am an ethnic minority achievement adviser – and much more besides. I am a daughter, granddaughter, sister, aunt, cousin, British, African and Caribbean, a member of the community. Although I spend much of my time in the world of education, it is my heritage, not my professional title and position, that is central to my identity. My family name tells me my place in Caribbean history. To be disconnected from that identity means losing not only the capacity to explain who I am to others but also the possibility of truly knowing myself.

After that visit to Ghana, I understood more deeply the importance of a strong positive community with a secure cultural base, a context which allows children to enter our changing world confident about who they are and their potential. If we have a strong community then we will have stronger young people and a stronger society. The key word 'community' includes the family, school, sport and interest groups, shared meeting places, the church, hairdressers and society in general – all the people who accompany and watch over young people on their life journey.

The adapted African proverb which opens this chapter expresses the truth that without society, without attention and support, pupils cannot strive, flourish and be successful. Parents and carers naturally play the major role in raising children, but they are not solely responsible. One of the most important factors for a pupil's success is whether adults beyond school are supporting and keeping track of them.

> When schools, families, and communities work together to support learning, children tend to do better in school, stay in school longer, and go on to higher education.

This was what the pupils told us during our research. It is through the pupils' voices that we have gained insight into the crucial part played by adults within and beyond the family.

Parents often have high aspirations for themselves and their children and regard education as very important. Key documents: The DfES's *Aiming High*, the Ofsted Handbook, and the Primary Strategy, *Excellence and Enjoyment*, point to the importance of involving parents and carers in the education process. The pupils we interviewed all had a strong idea of what success meant to them and of the part their parents played in their progress. Some talked about their parents as their role models and told us how they were supported by them in achieving their goals. They said it was important for pupils to be encouraged and pushed to be successful. They thought it was very hard for Black young people to find a way back if they 'lose their way' and that without family support it was difficult to get back on track.

Many of the pupils hoped that they would be the first in their family to attend university.

> 'success is being able to get into university...'

The interviewees saw higher education as their goal but they were anxious about what career path to follow. They felt they needed more guidance on careers. Several talked about the pressures on high achieving pupils and their concern lest they disappointed parents, teachers and the wider community.

Much of what they said belied the longstanding myth of parental apathy and lack of concern or involvement. Indeed some pupils talked about the additional educational opportunities organised for them by their parents – extra tutoring and supplementary school attendance.

It seems that what is needed is to develop more of a dialogue between schools and parents, a dialogue which creates genuine opportunities to share information, perceptions and ideas on an equal footing. Parents need to understand how systems work. They need to be given insight into their children's progress and invited to participate in decisions about their schooling and to contribute to school life. Parental involvement can also inspire communities to support the schools. Programmes established to encourage participation are not, however, always successful. Research by Blair (2001) and Crozier (2000) indicates that Black parents are generally less involved than other parents in school life.

There are almost as many reasons for parents appearing reluctant to show active interest in the life of the school as there are children! When I made informal contact with the parents, some of the reasons for this emerged:

- mistrust of teachers and of a system which has failed the parents in their own schooling
- parental involvement programmes which are often designed with a female home-based carer in mind and are inappropriate for working parents who cannot attend meetings or events during the day
- parental involvement being measured largely by whether parents work as classroom volunteers, actively participate in the PTA, and attend teacher-parent conferences. Little attention is paid to their role in the wider community and community schools and their family responsibilities
- parents' own negative experience of school

- pressures at work and elsewhere
- the problem that information about parents and homes is often gained at second hand and then filtered through the schools' concept of what constitutes a 'good parent'
- parents feeling isolated and lacking the confidence to approach schools for support for their children
- parents feeling that they are not wanted in school
- lack of information or understanding about how to volunteer their support
- lack of familiarity with the school language or jargon
- that the main relationship with the school is a negative one; parents are only contacted when there is a problem
- that Black parents find it particularly difficult to work with the secondary school if it has no culture of parental involvement
- successful parents' fear of being labelled as 'high maintenance' or 'aggressive' if they are closely involved with their children's education. They worry that teachers might develop a negative attitude towards them or their children.
- parents experiencing the difficult effects of generation gap and culture gap. They can feel at a loss when communicating with a teenager.

The pupils we interviewed were clear about the way forward. They advised that parents have to be made to believe in themselves as they help their children in school activities. Parents need to feel confident about communicating with teachers and working with them to forge a way forward. They also need to engage with their children's priorities, hopes and concerns. In the interviews, the pupils commended much of what their parents were doing for them and recommended approaches and further action:

- listen to and talk with your child
- be knowledgeable about the way the school operates and its success – 'When I wasn't doing very well, my mum checked out the league tables and then moved me...'
- have a strong interest in your child's education – 'My mum is always pushing me ... she makes sacrifices for me and I can't let it go to waste'
- motivate and encourage children to succeed
- give support and advice at times of change

- discuss dealing with the pressure of racism and street culture
- know about the issues that are key for 21st century youth
- link with outside support groups
- map out a school and career path, make an action plan and update it regularly
- have a good understanding of the influence of the media on young people

Some Black parents are looking for the order, discipline and overt religious values as taught in church schools. This strong religious orientation is seen by some Black families as a two-fold strength. Firstly, the church serves as a kind of extended family, providing material, human and ideological support for the bringing up and socialization of children. Secondly, religious values offer a framework – a unifying thread and ethos for the community. Many of the students said their parents had explicitly chosen single sex or church schools for their children as they regarded them as being stricter and more disciplined than other schools and believed their educational standards to be higher.

Interestingly, the pupils interviewed in the girls' school talked far less about social and street culture pressures. The pupils in both single sex schools said that the presence of the opposite sex would have been a distraction from learning. In order to succeed they had, they said, to choose their priorities and stick to them.

At single sex school you don't have to conform to gender stereotypes so much – 'I made the decision to continue with education and socialise less.'

There is widespread peer pressure, they felt, to resist succeeding academically. Many pupils talked about the pressures of the street culture to earn money and develop a 'bad' reputation. 'You see other people making money while you are still in education... It is a big temptation ... some of (my) other friends are doing dodgy stuff.'

They talked about how some of the pupils whose families are unstable see the street gangs as a family, and how some pupils use the power of the streets gangs to counteract the racism and the belittling experiences they endure. Several of the pupils talked about recognising turning points in their lives and how they had, with advice and support, made important decisions that kept them on course.

> 'A lot of people told me that I should not hang around with them if I want to go far in life.'
>
> '... I have more friends who have the right attitude ... the majority of my friends are into education or something that is positive.'

Parents are themselves gradually taking the opportunity to become more actively involved in education as teaching assistants, mentors, governors and support workers. These new professionals are saying that they want to do something to ensure the next generation have a better educational experience than they themselves did. They know about the challenges – and barriers – that pupils face along the educational path and in the competition for places in college and in careers.

Increasingly, secondary schools in Enfield are recognising the importance of parental involvement and are embarking on exciting and innovative projects. They are celebrating the achievement and successes of their Black pupils and developing a dialogue with parents and carers. There is still a way to go but progress is being made. Currently schools are

- making home visits
- sharing information and working in partnership seminars and conferences
- linking with community groups
- working with external agencies to run seminars on child development
- providing seminars on Black studies and culture
- working with libraries and museums
- running after school projects
- pioneering DfES funded projects
- keeping up with the children's learning
- offering community classes for parents and children
- offering mentoring programmes
- targeting particular groups – dads, grandparents, successful community group leaders – as well as mums
- linking with supplementary schools and heritage language organisations

Dreamcatcher and Workspeak

Local projects such as Dreamcatcher and Workspeak have been remarkably successful. Working with schools, Ethnic Minority Achievement Advisers and the Enfield Business Partnership have set out to broaden the horizons of pupils from ethnic minority backgrounds in Key Stages 2, 3 and 4. A key feature of these projects has been introducing role models from the pupils' own communities to challenge stereotypical career choices and motivate pupils to strive for rewarding futures. Pupils say in their evaluations how inspiring they found the presentations and discussions.

Partnership conferences

Partnership conferences, an annual event in Enfield, are designed to enable discussion about the achievement of ethnic minority pupils. They take place between teachers, governors, parents, advisers, mentors, community organisations, the mayor and the director of education. The prime focus is on how the links between parties can be strengthened to share good practice and celebrate achievement. Each conference features several guest speakers and there are workshops which explore areas of interest. An award ceremony is held for ethnic minority pupils nominated by the schools and there are performances by pupils.

Developing links with community schools

We value the work of supplementary and mother tongue schools as key partners in education and are committed to developing creative partnerships with community groups in order to enrich and extend the experiences of our pupils in line with DfEE (1999) recommendations. Community Learning in Schools brings the many learning providers in the minority communities in Enfield into a productive network that provides a range of services to schools that meet the community's needs. Schools are redefined as not just part of the community but as part of a community school model that is fully inclusive. The objective is to build an effective partnership with our community groups so we can share resources and strategies in ways that will encourage our children to achieve educationally while still maintaining their positive cultural identities.

Stand up to Racism

> Successful schools ensure that parents are treated as equal partners in education for their children ... they try and find imaginative ways to break down barriers and make parents welcome, being responsive to parents' needs and respectful of the constraints upon them. (DfES, 2002)

In response to requests from schools for support in developing their Race Equality policies, EMA Advisers within the School Improvement Service set up Stand up to Racism. The sessions enabled all staff to consider how best to address the statutory duties to report, record and deal with racist incidents and also how to develop a proactive approach, using the curriculum to encourage positive attitudes to ethnic differences, cultural diversity and racial equality among the school community.

The sessions allowed school staff to explore their own beliefs and attitudes about ethnic minority communities so they could examine previously unexamined prejudices about people from ethnic and class backgrounds which differ from their own. Also explored were ways of working with all parents and the school community to challenge racism and break down barriers, especially in mainly white schools. It is impossible to have an island of excellence in a sea of community indifference

> **Parents' forum**
> Parents agree that the parental involvement in their children's work is essential but they do not always share the same understanding of how that this might be best achieved. (DfES, 2003)

Some schools are organising forums for parents to network with other parents, explore involvement in education and tackle any barriers. One of the areas highlighted in secondary schools is communication. Some schools have addressed this issue by formalising links with parents using bilingual teachers and support staff and employing a home-school liaison worker. Home-school liaison officers not only support parents new to the school but also organise parent education workshops, operate homework hotlines, arrange home visits, and recruit and work with parent volunteers. Parents are a rich fund of talent. Conducting surveys to identify the skills and experience that parents have and the kind of volunteer work they might wish to do has been practically helpful and illuminating.

Parent mentoring programme

We have several examples of parents and schools working together to create the right environment so that the entire school community can feel valued and have confidence and self-esteem. These schools have developed mentoring programmes for the students and mentors – and also for the parents who are mentoring other parents. These prove most successful when they have a clearly structured agreement between school, parents, community groups and pupils that includes professional development programmes, parental support workshops, resource and video libraries and ICT proficiency classes.

Celebrating Black History Month

The celebration of Black History Month each October is one illustration of working in partnership in a practical and highly effective way. The schools display their work across the borough in its libraries, art gallery and museum. The creative partnership formed between education providers, libraries, an art gallery, the museum and the Black community develops shared understandings and a sense of one cohesive learning community right across the borough.

Enfield is committed to working in partnership with parents and the wider community to raise the achievement of pupils in our multi-ethnic schools. Because we want to build a safe, caring and creative environment, we need to own the vision of joint responsibility in which everyone is clear about their roles and is working towards common goals according to common principles. The key principles are those that foster traditional community values of partnership, the sense of truth, justice and doing things for and taking care of others. Our vision is strengthened by the Race Relations Amendment Act and its emphasis on developing trust, working in partnership, sharing responsibility and ensuring equality of opportunity. My work has also been inspired by Maud Blair and Jenny Bourne's project for the DfES *Making the Difference* (1998).

The Ofsted Handbook of 2003 also offers wise guidance:

> The most effective schools were listening schools which took time to talk with students and parents; which were prepared to consider and debate value...
>
> In very good schools the parents are involved in schools. They are consulted extensively and their views are taken into account to bring about improvement.

It does indeed take a whole village to raise a child. We should think of children as village-raised – mothered, fathered, fed, clothed, protected and nurtured – children with a secure sense of identity, who are loved and taught by everyone in the village. The success of our children is largely dependent on the success of the village to work in partnership, share responsibility, listen to each other and work together to solve problems and overcome barriers. Success is achieved interdependently; no one accomplishes anything without the help of others.

Nelson Mandela says it for us all:

> Our road to the glorious future lies through collective hard work to accomplish the objectives of creating a people centred society.

9

BILINGUAL, BLACK AND GIFTED

John Broadbent

There is a poem by the Czech writer Miroslav Holub which encourages us to take comfort in the fact that 'so many people have heads'. The kind of head he is talking about is clearly a child's head, one with an irrepressible ability to imagine a different world with 'an entirely new bird', 'an entirely new hare', 'an entirely new bumble-bee' as well as 'a project for doing away with piano lessons'.

Adventurous thinkers and writers

In a classroom in a North London school, an English translation of these thoughts was displayed inside a drawing of a child's head, and a specially invited group of Year 7 pupils were encouraged to exercise writing skill and empathy by imagining different worlds for themselves. The pupils produced their own versions of the original idea. One pupil drew the head of a cat and began her poem:

> In it there is a crafty plan.
> A way of getting two dinners.

Another saw things from inside a scientist's head:

> In it there's questions not yet answered.
> And places not been step-foot on.

Another child got inside a mother's head:

> In it there is the breakfast waiting to be made.
> The children do not help

The pupils showed their ability to use Holub's work as a source of inspiration and a model. They put themselves inside the heads of people or animals and described the thoughts, ideas, dreams they imagined for them. Their poems were the outcome of a project aimed at challenging pupils to experiment with writing and particularly with poetry.

This Adventurous Writers Project was part of one school's provision for its gifted and talented pupils. It ran workshop sessions for pupils who had attained high scores in National Curriculum tests and other reading tests and who could be expected to respond well to demanding and imaginative literary tasks conducted in a small group. Pupils known to have high ability in languages other than English were encouraged to attend. All those involved were invited to bring a friend if they wanted, so as to counter the notion of an elite or favoured group. The intention was to meet the combined needs initially of the most motivated as well as the most able pupils, who might then be relied upon to sustain their experimentation with writing autonomously in private or, more advantageously, providing an audience for one another.

To ensure that ethnic minority pupils were fully represented in the initial group, school data on ethnicity was used in selecting the participants. So the 'adventurous writers' group had pupils in it from a range of cultural and linguistic backgrounds who were achieving highly within their own ethnic group. Some of them had scored highly in non-verbal tests of cognitive ability, indicating their potential to make good progress generally when given appropriate challenge and support. Among them was a boy who spoke French and Arabic and who had begun his UK education in Year 4. He wrote a poem in French and, with help, translated it into English.

Poets, poems, language, identity

Several of the poems studied as a stimulus by the creative writing group were written originally in a language other than English and available in translation. The pupils, many of whom were bilingual, were encouraged to share and extend their knowledge of language and languages. In another project, 'Drama into Text', led by the Literacy Strategy manager working with EMA advisers, pupils have been brought closer to texts through visual images and related dramatic activities. The general standards of writing have been significantly raised by these projects and the highest performers have also improved within the general rising tide. We have shown that there is no reason why newly arriving refugees and their classmates may not aspire to the levels of attainment described in the National Curriculum Attainment Targets as 'Exceptional Performance' in English, whereby

> pupils' writing has shape and impact and shows control of a range of styles maintaining the interest of the reader throughout. Narratives use structure as well as vocabulary for a range of imaginative effects, and non-fiction is coherent, reasoned and persuasive. A variety of grammatical constructions and punctuation is used accurately and appropriately and with sensitivity. (The National Curriculum handbook, 1999)

These are goals for all pupils to aim for, not just the seemingly most able. The same is true about the criteria for awarding A* and A grades in GCSE examinations in English and the languages pupils bring with them into the classroom. There need be no upper limits to the capabilities to be catered for and elicited, nor to the opportunities for finding attuned audiences. There is, for example, an annual award to a young person under 18 in *The Times* Stephen Spender Prize for poetry translation. Eyre (1997) outlines two possible models for identifying talent: an exclusive model which essentially defines, identifies and provides for pupils, and an inclusive model which provides, recognises ability and evaluates plans accordingly. 'Schools', he suggests, 'become more effective in identifying able children as they get better at providing for them'.

Making connections with complementary forms of intelligence

Working with poetry means that learners of English as an additional language have a real challenge. If given the right support, they will eventually be able to use English and their other languages for a wide range of purposes including creative expression. But initially they may display their capabilities in other than linguistic ways, notably via kinaesthetic awareness or physical prowess, or in terms of visual, technological and musical artistry.

Research I undertook in 1985 for the European Commission defined three distinct levels of linguistic development among emerging bilingual pupils, and looked at the purposes to which they put each language in their repertoire. At the earliest stages of acquiring a new language, learners start out by memorising elements of language for *transactional* purposes. As they become more fluent and able to use the new language for thought, the language resources at their command begin to meet *reflective* purposes. They may even start to dream or talk to themselves in the newer language.

Many of the young people interviewed as part of the EC Project on Community Languages in the Secondary Curriculum were aware that the scope of the language they had learned from their families was largely insufficient for educational or vocational purposes. The summit of achievement does not begin to be reached until pupils are able to use two of their languages for *creative performance* purposes – for telling a story or joke, writing poetry or constructing a persuasive argument.

The pupils whose linguistic knowledge and use was under scrutiny were in English-medium schools and were striving to maintain their connections with their families' languages of Italian, Panjabi or Urdu. The three levels of language use defined by the EU project can equally usefully be applied to the Turkish speakers in Enfield schools who are learning English – and to bilingual learners elsewhere. Kathy Coulthard's research (2003) shows that when given opportunities to engage with complex visual texts in a supportive learning environment bilingual pupils progress well. Given a safe and stimulating context, they demonstrate their ability to communicate complex thoughts in English.

Work done in a number of Enfield schools suggests that there are many young people who perform well in non-verbal tests but not in verbal tests. These pupils may be excellent at representational drawing, technology and ICT but may still have difficulty expressing themselves orally. Not all such pupils are working in an unfamiliar language. There are English monolinguals who also benefit from working through activities where there is incremental cognitive demand but where the context is engineered to supply substantial clues for comprehension and scaffolding for the production of relevant language. Cummins (1989), who has investigated bilingual education in Canada, and Deryn Hall (1995) suggest how this 'context embeddedness' can be achieved in practice.

When offering pupils the opportunity to interact with successful peers in learning experiences which will also be of value to these peers, it is wise to start with tasks which are firmly embedded in a recognisable context. The National Curriculum offers plenty of opportunities for this kind of support, often accompanied by predictable forms of language use, such as those found in science experiments or geography fieldwork. All the pupils generally require are models of effective communication that link the concepts they need to absorb and manipulate.

Emotional Intelligence

Verbal ability is closely connected with social ability. How effectively children interact positively with others depends largely on their ability to participate in activities involving peers – or even to organise and develop activities of this kind. The DfES has expressed interest in work led in several Enfield schools on the development of emotional intelligence. One local Gifted and Talented Co-ordinator has written about this and describes how he uses the ideas of Michael Brearley (2001).

Daniel Goleman (1996), who has evolved the concept of emotional intelligence, has argued that it is necessary for the efficient development of all other forms of intelligent and creative functioning in human beings. Because of their responsibilities of caring for their siblings or perhaps interpreting and mediating for their parents in challenging contexts, many of the children growing up in socio-economically disadvantaged communities may be far more emotionally intelligent than we give them credit for.

We are currently seeking to find out how successful learners achieve what they do. One pupil of African origin who is now in the sixth form of an Enfield school but who started his GCSE courses in a most unpromising way, is one of those who agreed to be interviewed. He described some of the processes which had combined to help him turn the vicious circle of rejection and intellectual decline into a virtuous spiral of escalating achievement. He described how:

- the Head of Year 10 had noted his increasing disaffection and had put aside considerable time for trying to change his negative attitudes towards his teachers and the teachers' negative attitudes towards him
- the Science teacher had decided to give him and a number of his disruptive peers another chance and had kept them back after school to go through the concepts associated with the circulation of the blood. When the group failed to understand the explanations and diagrams, the teacher rearranged the desks in the rooms to simulate the valves and ventricles of the heart, and organised the pupils to move through the different chambers so that they came to understand physically how the process worked
- several of the pupils, some of whom were relatively successful athletes, began to take an interest in biology, and changed their friendship patterns in the course of exploring the subject and sharing notes about their discoveries.

It was impressive that this young man was so aware of the factors that had made a significant difference to his eventual achievements. He observed that:

- several teachers had cared enough to think through his situation with him and to provide some kinaesthetic ways for finding a foothold in study
- some of his fellow students had included him in a new peer group of successful learners.

Work in Enfield in sports education acknowledges the dimension of developing attitudes, towards oneself and others and towards learning and achievement, in ways which draw heavily on understandings of emotional intelligence, or perhaps more precisely on emotional literacy, which is composed of the teachable skills involved.

The Junior Athlete Education programme of the Youth Sport Trust also offers models and analogies that work for several different intelligences and other areas of the curriculum. The programme recognises that success in sport, like success in most other forms of endeavour, depends on collective support, so the emphasis is on building a 'Team You' (a group of people who will provide joined-up support and guidance – parents, peers, coach, mentor, teacher) and on individual or group mentoring. The programme adopts a rational approach to lifestyle management, encouraging pupils to see what is important at different times of the year and at different times in their lives, so they can balance any over-riding interest in a sport. And performance is profiled in a way that allows young athletes to plan the stages by which they can come closer to their imagined model of performance.

Complementing these approaches are the deliberate attempts made across several curriculum areas by Enfield schools to help pupils establish connections between the different subject categories into which their knowledge falls. One initiative encouraged groups of pupils to explore the expression encountered in works of art through dance sequences; the project 'Drama into Text' already mentioned provided pupils with examples of art work such as 'The Journey of the Magi'. The pupils interpreted this image dramatically before moving on to read T S Eliot's poem of the same name.

Capitalising on capabilities arising from cognitive dissonance

The adults involved in the Adventurous Writers' Project were pleased but not unduly surprised at the thoughtful and imaginative outcomes of the creative writing club. It seems reasonable to assume that young people growing up in contexts in which they are required to use more than one language – and perhaps more than two – and who have to struggle harder for social acceptance than most adolescents do, will, if adequately encouraged, ultimately perform better than their monolingual peers for whom acceptance has come more easily. For many pupils the difficulty of learning English and the problems of coping with racism and prejudice may prove almost insuperable. They need a climate in which they can construct a sense of collective self-confidence alongside other empathetic pupils. They need opportunities to clarify their linguistic, cultural and emotional experiences. But every one of them is likely to reach a point at which they overtake their monolingual peers in some way.

It seems likely that growing up with access to more than one complete system of grammatical structure, analogy and cultural experience can provide a stimulus for reflection and for resolving contrasts, quite apart from the recently reported work (*The Times* 14/6/2004) on the retention by bilinguals of mental abilities into old age. George Steiner (2001) exemplifies this mental faculty. He describes his life as a process of translation, as he moved between the different languages in which he was fluent. He grew up in Paris after his family fled from Austria. He drew on his experience to construct a convincing theory of literary culture. He argues that the best novels of the 20th century – by Conrad, Kafka, Nabokov, Rushdie – were created at the boundaries of national or cultural convention, where value systems come into conflict. And Edward de Bono, another who grew up in a multilingual context, can claim to be one of the few people who have had a major impact on the way we think.

Developing theory and policy

Enfield's published policy for gifted and talented pupils takes account of the links between intellect, social ability and linguistic range. It considers general rationale, definitions and identification:

> ...we define 'gifted and talented' pupils as those children who possess demonstrated or potential abilities which, when encouraged by teaching, resources and learning opportunities, will be evidenced in high performance in areas such as intellectual, creative, specific academic, psychomotor or leadership ability or in the visual and performing arts.
>
> These are children who require qualitatively differentiated learning opportunities and programmes beyond the regular school programme so they can fully realise their abilities and their potential contributions to their communities.

Enfield's policy chimes in with those of Westminster, Haringey and Kensington and Chelsea. The Gifted and Talented Co-ordinator in Holland Park Comprehensive School is reported to use Renzulli's 'Revolving Door' model as we do: to identify underachieving pupils for whom English is an additional language. For examples of successes achieved by this method, see National Association for Gifted Children (2003) and a more detailed account appears in Renzulli (1973).

The Adventurous Writers' project was run in a large multilingual school in Enfield, a partner in the Excellence in Cities programme. The project is committed to the policy and practice of educational inclusion, which aims to make effective educational provision for all pupils including those defined as gifted and talented. One key approach to improving provision is to focus on one designated group of pupils at a time – African Caribbean boys perhaps, or Somali girls, or maybe the most able athletes or the most able musicians or mathematicians – to determine how the specific provision can be built around their needs and enthusiasms while also being inspirational for the other pupils and teachers.

We needed a theory which was inclusive in its understanding of how the brain functions in relation to the many different aspects of success. We wanted to build on the wide range of strengths and enthusiasms of our pupils in ways which would inspire them to concentrate and work hard. We found it in the work of Howard Gardner on Multiple Intelligences. Gardner (1983) emphasises the socially conditioned dimensions of ability and success: 'Intelligence is the ability to solve problems, or create products, that are valued within one or more cultural setting.'

Gardner first developed his approach to widening the prevailing understandings about intelligence for the Project on Human Potential based at the Harvard Graduate School of Education in the 1980s. This ambitious project sought to assess the state of knowledge about human potential and its realisation. Some important findings emerged. Gardner's contribution lay in the application of contemporary neuroscience to the educational processes that operate in schools. Starting with an analysis of differential impact of brain damage on musicality and language, he identified seven distinct intelligences. Only the first two of these are generally examined in our national assessment systems, even though all have a place in the National Curriculum from the Foundation Stage onwards. The seven intelligences are:

- linguistic
- logical/mathematical
- intra-personal
- interpersonal
- bodily kinaesthetic
- spatial
- musical

Linguistic intelligence is expressed in the areas of learning for the Foundation Stage as 'communication, language and literacy'. 'Logical/mathematical intelligence' may be approached through a combination of 'knowledge and understanding of the world' and 'mathematical development'. Intra-personal and interpersonal intelligences are together represented in 'personal, social and emotional development'. Bodily kinaesthetic intelligence relates to 'physical development'. Creative development encompasses both 'spatial' and 'musical' intelligences.

In a later work, Gardner (1999) identifies the activities in the school curriculum which may best stimulate the interaction of the different forms of intelligence. He analyses the possibilities of a museum visit, for example, and a project on the Holocaust. He endorses the practice of providing activities outside the conventional curriculum to certain pupils, before bringing similar activities into the mainstream. This does not conflict with Enfield's advice to consultants and the Ethnic Minority Achievement advisers to work mainly with mainstream classes. The gifted and talented strand has made a case for greater additional challenge in the classroom and also for 'school action plus' in catering for the more able pupils. Having a writer in residence is one strategy for providing school action plus, but the writer must also be a good teacher. It is better still to encourage EMA consultants and classroom practitioners to develop their own skills as poets and learners of languages and share their skills with their pupils.

Provision for the gifted and talented

To sum up, provision should build on the existing strengths of pupils, by

- increasing the range of choices in terms of the learning activities proposed to pupils, based on recognised potential
- starting with context-embedded learning but increasing intellectual challenge and removing ceilings to achievement
- bringing ideas from extra-curricular provision into the mainstream
- turning features commonly identified as 'problems' into distinct advantages – cultural hyphenation, bilingualism, cognitive dissonance, and critical thinking
- resolving dilemmas around grouping and differentiated levels of performance in a single classroom
- focusing on the achievements of advanced EAL students and competent bilinguals
- debating, creative writing, journalism and the use and study of other media leading to aesthetic production (see also Winstanley, 2004)

Evaluation procedures need to determine what works or doesn't work in raising achievement and requires

- analysing data on performance and progression
- keeping records of exceptional work in portfolios and details of how it was achieved, in terms of opportunities and forms of support offered, in ongoing extensions to schemes of work
- interviewing staff and learners, and bringing their perspectives together
- writing up cameos of research into educational development (because there is little or no research relating to effectiveness in this area)

The Gifted and Talented Co-ordinators funded through Excellence in Cities and the consultants funded through the Ethnic Minority Achievement Grant seek to share and disseminate the values that underpin Enfield's approach to highly able pupils – essentially, intolerance of low expectations and belief in teamwork. We work together to

- raise aspirations as to what an intercultural, multilingual context can offer to learners and to society in general
- create an inclusive environment outside of the normal classroom, and often outside of the normal curricular and pastoral structures of the school, and then re-import the outcomes back into the mainstream
- share views with pupils, colleagues, parents and others about what seems to work and what clearly doesn't
- exchange knowledge and skills across the multiple capabilities of a range of different forms of professional expertise.

By working in this way, we hope to give all our pupils the chance to discover their own potential and work with their teachers to develop it to the full.

With thanks to Penny Travers for sharing outcomes from the 'Adventurous writers project'.

AFTERWORD
BEING GIVEN A CHANCE

Gillian Klein

We all know the sad stories, and there are statistics galore to bear them out. They go something like this:

> Eager infants gleefully going to school
>
> Children gobbling up the knowledge their primary schools offer them and effortlessly developing a wealth of skills
>
> Sparky and bright, off they go to secondary school
>
> And then it all goes wrong. By year 9 disenchantment has set in. Some children slide sullenly through the rest of the statutory school provision and come out with their promise unfulfilled. Some become wholly disaffected – and another set of statistics – this lot for the Home Office – indicates what happens to these young people.

Good practice is not a rarity in secondary schools. But secondary schools, unlike primary, are departmentalised, sectioned. That is the nature of the beast. Not only does this create problems for the schools but it also inhibits the sharing of good practice beyond the school.

My work in education has – for more years than I care to think about – been about identifying good practice that affords pupils, especially ethnic minority pupils, an optimal educational opportunity. Identifying good practice and the thinking behind it, and disseminating it as widely as possible. And good practice, as a Black high achiever says here, is about 'being given a chance'.

Initially my job was to seek out the good examples and make them known; now as a publisher, I try to identify the gaps in documented good practice and find the people who can fill them. Trentham is one of several publishers that has produced useful books on equality and excellence in primary practice. But relevant and up-to-date books on the secondary sector are rare across the market. And most of those are written by academics, who are driven by the Research Assessment Exercise rather than the needs of schools.

So I knew what I was looking for – what Trentham's constituency would be looking for – a book about good practice in secondary schools written by the professionals who are shaping it. It would have to have a unified vision and a coherent approach. A good way to achieve coherence is to focus on a single local education authority. Trentham has published several books set in a single authority, two of them in London boroughs. Another LEA with a record of enlightened practice is the London borough of Enfield. And working as one of the Ethnic Minority Achievement advisers is Penny Travers.

I knew Penny through the leading edge work that the EMA team does, so I asked her to write the book. 'No' said Penny, 'I can't write it. It needs others to write chapters for it.' Impatient for the book, I warned her that it's harder to edit a book than to write it yourself – so she roped me in to help.

Readers won't be interested in the process we've been through, unless they're planning to do something similar themselves, so I won't dwell on it. But Penny and I had an initial meeting and later a follow-up discussion with the writing team – and all have delivered. This is the first time some of them have written for general publication. They have bravely – and generously – moved out of the parameters of the jobs they do so well to respond to a totally new challenge. And they have given you, the readers, a vivid picture of what works for secondary pupils – for refugees, Roma, Black high achievers, a group of Somali low achievers, the gifted and talented, and emerging and developing bilinguals – and how this can be realised. They have explained why certain things were done, as well as how. Our thanks go to them all. And my thanks to Penny for her sustained encouragement and support of the authors, as well as her own work on the book.

I believe in this book. First, the content: the chapters are excellent – exciting work clearly described and reflected on, that will be directly useful to teachers and advisers in the UK and beyond and will help enhance the educational experience of their own pupils.

Secondly: transferability. Trentham's list began with a book produced in and for Maidenhead Teachers' Centre in the 1980s. I knew why it would succeed – the key was that everything being done to support language learning there was transferable well beyond the generating authority. This is true also of the book you are holding now.

Thirdly, coherence. The specificity of a context generates a clear picture. Combine relevant content and a coherent message with transferability to other schools, other regions and, in some cases, other countries and we have a recipe for a really useful publication.

But what I also learned from that initial project, now long out of print, is this: a book created along these parameters will by its nature be state of the art. The initiatives described will run their course, the authors will develop new projects, the pupils will move through and others will take their place creating other priorities, the political goalposts will be shifted (they always are), the social context will shift too. New issues will arise, requiring new books to be written.

But for the moment we have a fine, functional, if not perfect wheel. By all means adapt it, dear readers, but there's no need to reinvent it. Roll with Enfield's model for as long as it takes you where you want to go. And when you *do* need to reshape it significantly, please let Trentham know!

References and further reading

Adhami M, Johnson, D and Shayer, M (1998) *Thinking maths. The programme for accelerated learning in mathematics. CAME project.* London: Heinemann

Association for the Teaching of Mathematics (1993) *Talking maths, talking language.* Derby: ATM

Barnes D, Britton J and Rosen H (1969) *Language, the learner and the school.* Harmondsworth: Penguin

Berry J (2004) *Only one of ME: selected poems*. London, Macmillan

Blair M (2001) *Why pick on me? School exclusion and Black youth.* Stoke on Trent: Trentham Books

Blair M and Bourne J (1998) *Making the difference; teaching and learning in successful multi-ethnic schools.* Sudbury: DfEE and Open University Press

Brearley, M (2001) *Emotional Intelligence in the Classroom: creative learning strategies for 11s-18.* Carmarthen: Crown House Publishing

Broadbent J (1987) *The Inclusion of Community Languages in the Normal Curricular Arrangements of Local Education Authority Maintained Schools in England and Wales: the 1984-1987 Report of the EC Pilot Project: Community Languages in the Secondary Curriculum.* London: University of London Institute of Education

Coulthard K (2003) 'The words to say it' young bilingual pupils responding to visual texts in *Children Reading Pictures.* Arizpe E and Styles M (2003) London: Routledge

Cummins J (1989) Language and Literacy Acquisition in Bilingual Contexts. *Journal of Multicultural and Multilingual Development* Vol. 6, No. 5

Cummins J (1996) *Negotiating Identities: education for empowerment in a diverse society.* Ontario: CABE

Dadzie S (2000) *Toolkit for Tackling Racism in Schools.* Stoke on Trent: Trentham Books

DES (Department of Education) (1985) *Education for All: the report of the inquiry into the education of children from ethnic minority groups* (Swann Report). London: HMSO

DFEE (Department for Education and Employment) (1999) *Excellence in Cities.* London: The Stationery Office

DFEE (2001) *KS3 National Strategy English department training.* DFEE 0234/2001

DFEE (2001) *KS3 National Strategy Literacy across the curriculum.* DFEE 0235

DFEE (2001) *KS3 National Strategy Framework for teaching mathematics Years 7, 8 and 9.* DFEE 0020/2001

DFEE (2001) *KS3 National Strategy Raising aspects of ethnic minority achievement.* DFEE 0689/2001

DfES (Department for Education and Skills) (2002) *KS3 National Strategy Access and engagement in mathematics.* DfES 0251/2002

DfES (2002) *KS3 National Strategy Training materials for the foundation subjects.* DfES 0530/2002

DfES (2003) *KS3 National Strategy Key messages: Pedagogy and practice.* DfES 0125/2003

DfES (Department for Education and Skills) (2002) *Removing the Barriers.* London: DfES

DfES (2003) *Aiming high: raising the achievement of African-Caribbean pupils.* London: DfES

DfES(2003) *Excellence and Enjoyment – a strategy for primary schools.* London: DfES

DfES (2004) *Aiming high: Understanding the Educational needs of Minority Ethnic pupils in mainly white schools.* DfES May 2004

Demetr N G, Bessnov N V, Kutenkov, V K Istoria Tsygan (2000) *Novy Vzglyad* [Romany History, new approach] Voronezh: Russian Academy of Science

Enfield (1999) *Enabling Progress in multilingual classrooms 1999.* LCAS London Borough of Enfield

Enfield (2002) *Striving to Succeed – an exploration of the reasons for the disproportionate exclusion rate of black African-Caribbean pupils from Enfield schools* (2002) LCAS, School Improvement Service London borough of Enfield

European Roma Rights Centre (1999) *A Special Remedy: Roma and schools for the mentally handicapped in the Czech Republic.* Budapest: ERRC

European Roma Rights Centre (2001) *State of Impunity: Human right abuse of Roma in Romania.* Budapest: ERRC

Eyre D (1997) *Able Children in Ordinary Schools.* London: David Fulton

Gardner H (1983) *Frames of Mind* (second ed 1993). London: Collins Fontana

Gardner H (1999) *Intelligence Reframed: multiple intelligences for the 21st century.* New York: Basic Books

Gillborn D and Mirza H S (2000) *Educational Inequality: mapping race, class and gender.* London: Ofsted

Goleman D (1996) *Emotional Intelligence, why it can matter more than IQ.* London: Bloomsbury

Green P (1999) *Raise the Standard...successful policy and practice in cities across the European Community.* Stoke on Trent: Trentham Books

Hall D (1995) *Assessing the Needs of Bilingual Pupil.* London: David Fulton

Hart S (1991) The collaborative dimension – risks and rewards of collaboration. In C McLaughlin and M Rouse (eds) *Supporting Schools.* London: David Fulton

Holub, M (2002) *Skvosty poezie.* Prague: Odeon Press, Vydala Euromedia Group k.s.

Ingmire, S (2000) Does God love Roma? *The Month,* Nov 2000, p423

Kahin M (1997) *Educating Somali Children in Britain.* Stoke on Trent: Trentham Books

Macpherson W et al (1999) *The Stephen Lawrence Inquiry.* London: the Stationery Office

Meek M (1991) *On being literate.* London Bodley Head

National Advisory Committee on Creative and Cultural Education (1999) *All our Futures: Creativity, Culture and Education.* DfEE

National Association for Gifted Children (2003) *Meeting Needs of Pupils with English as an Additional Language: some practical guidance.* Milton Keynes: NAGC

Ofsted (1996) *Recent Research on the Achievement of Ethnic Minority Pupils* by D Gillborn and C Gipps London: HMSO

Ofsted (1999) *Raising the Attainment of Minority Ethnic Pupils.* London: Ofsted

Ofsted (2002) *Achievement of Black Caribbean Pupils: Good practice in secondary schools.* London: Ofsted

Ofsted (2003) *Inspecting Schools: Framework for inspecting schools, effective from September 2003.* London: Ofsted

Ofsted (2004) *Managing the Ethnic Minority Achievement Grant: good practice in secondary schools.* London: Ofsted

Osler A and Morrison M (2000) *Inspecting Schools for Race Equality: Ofsted's strengths and weaknesses. Report for the Commission for Racial Equality.* Stoke on Trent: Trentham Books and CRE

Renzulli J S (1973) Talent potential in minority group students in *Exceptional Children,* vol. 39, no.6, 1973, pp 437-44

Reay D and Mirza H S (2000) Black supplementary schools: spaces of radical blackness. In Majors R (ed) *The education of black children.* London: Falmer

Rutter J (2003) *Supporting refugee children in 21st Century Britain – a compendium of essential information* (new revised edition). Stoke on Trent: Trentham Books

Shan S-J and Bailey, P (1991) *Multiple Factors – classroom mathematics for equality and justice.* Stoke on Trent: Trentham books

Steiner G (2001) *Grammars of Creation.* London: Faber

Supple C (1999) *From Prejudice to Genocide: learning about the Holocaust* (revised ed). Stoke on Trent: Trentham

Tyler C (2005 forthcoming) *Traveller Education – accounts of good practice.* (Stoke on Trent: Trentham

White R and Gunstone R (1992) *Probing Understanding.* London: Falmer

Winstanley C (2004) *Too Clever by Half – a fair deal for gifted children.* Stoke on Trent: Trentham Books

Wray D and Lewis M (1997) *Extending Literacy.* London: Routledge

WWW.anc.org.za – Mandela speaks: speeches, statements and writing of Nelson Mandela 1950-2004

Notes on contributors

This book was conceived at a time when all the contributors worked in different roles for or with the education service in the London Borough of Enfield. Some have since moved on but all remain committed to collaboration and exploration within inclusive settings. All write here in a personal capacity.

John Broadbent is currently the Co-ordinator of the Gifted and Talented Strand of Excellence in Cities. He has a varied background in language teaching, school improvement, secondary headship and educational research.

Janet Campbell is an Ethnic Minority Achievement Adviser. She is a Primary specialist and is particularly interested in literacy development. She is currently working with the Department for Education and Skills to develop specialist training in English as an additional language for Teaching Assistants.

Mala German is an Educational Psychologist who has a specialist post working in the multidisciplinary Enfield Child Guidance Service Refugee Team. She is interested in promoting an awareness of the psychological strengths and needs of refugee children, families, unaccompanied minors and how a multi-agency approach can achieve effective support.

Alison Heap is an Ethnic Minority Achievement Adviser working mostly in secondary schools. She is interested in a wide range of areas including support for refugee and asylum-seeking pupils, underachieving groups, literacy development and whole school issues relating to race equality.

Lesley Higgs was Head of English in a secondary school for several years and is now a Key Stage 3 Teaching and Learning Consultant. She is interested in all aspects of inclusion and what inclusion means in practice.

Gillian Klein is co-founder and director of Trentham Books. She has written widely for educationalists and children, and is the founder and editor of the pratitioners' journal *Race Equality Teaching*, formerly *MCT Multicultural Teaching.*

Vasant Mahandru worked as an Ethnic Minority Achievement Adviser until December 2003. He has wide experience of research in linguistics, particularly comparative linguistics. He is interested in the use of language in mathematics and, in particular, the challenge it offers bilingual pupils.

Marcia Sinclair is an Ethnic Minority Achievement Adviser working cross phase with a particular focus on African Caribbean achievement. She has worked in education for over twenty years in a range of senior posts including Senco, deputy headteacher and ESOL lecturer. She has lived and taught in many countries including Spain, America and the Caribbean.

Deborah Thompson has taught English, History and Politics and is currently Literacy Strategy manager and acting Key Stage 3 manager. Her career has spanned teaching children in Reception classrooms to students at Key Stage 5, giving her a practical understanding of what is meant by continuity of good practice.

Penny Travers works as an Ethnic Minority Achievement Adviser. She is particularly interested in development work and in scaffolding the curriculum to support and challenge pupils and unleash creativity. She is currently carrying out action research with colleagues on more advanced bilingual pupils.

Giang Vo is a teacher in an inner city school. As a child she was aware that adults could have helped her more in some of the experiences she went through as a refugee. She contributed to this book to remind herself and us that she is now in a position to affect young people's lives in a very positive way.

Graham Went has been the Support Teacher for Travellers and Roma for seven years. Prior to this he was for twenty years the deputy, and then headteacher, of a primary school in Walthamstow, east London. Apart from a short spell teaching in the Falkland Islands, his 35 years in teaching have all been in city areas, and he is passionate about equality of opportunity for all.

Index